Exploring Geography in a
Changing World

3

Harry Leaver
9A x 2
9 HJO

Simon Ross

HODDER
EDUCATION
AN HACHETTE UK COMPANY

Hachette UK's policy is to use papers that are natural, renewable and recyclable products and made from wood grown in sustainable forests. The logging and manufacturing processes are expected to conform to the environmental regulations of the country of origin.

Orders: please contact Bookpoint Ltd, 130 Milton Park, Abingdon, Oxon OX14 4SB. Telephone: (44) 01235 827720. Fax: (44) 01235 400454. Lines are open 9.00–5.00, Monday to Saturday, with a 24-hour message answering service. Visit our website at www.hoddereducation.co.uk

| Impression number | 10 |
| Year | 2017 |

Cover photo © Sergio Pitamitz/Corbis
Illustrations by Barking Dog Art
Typeset in New Baskerville 11.5/13pt
Layouts by Amanda Easter
Printed in India

A catalogue record for this title is available from the British Library

ISBN: 978 0340 94606 0

Other titles in the series

Year 7 Pupil's Book: 978 0340 94607 7
Dynamic Learning 1: 978 1444 11631 1

Year 8 Pupil's Book: 978 0340 94605 3
Dynamic Learning 2: 978 1444 11775 2

Dynamic Learning 3: 978 1444 11776 9

CONTENTS

Acknowledgements

As always I am grateful to my family for their forbearance during the writing of this book together with the following individuals:

Keith Wheatley
Lydia Young
Pupils of 9X (2009–10)
Myrtle Plume
Tony Escritt
Hong Ki
The Florida Connection (Ann, Tony, Clare, Dave, Nikki, Sue and Penny)
Mostafa Shudafat (Badia Research and Development Centre, Jordan)

Dedication:

This book is dedicated to Elspeth Goate.

The Publishers would like to thank the following for permission to reproduce copyright material:

Photo credits:

p.1 Johnson Space Center/NASA; **p.6** NASA/SCIENCE PHOTO LIBRARY; **p.8** VINCENT THIAN/AP/Press Association Images; **p.9** © Simon Ross; **p.10** tl Sean Dempsey/PA Archive/Press Association Images, br © Simon Ross; **p.11** © Simon Ross; **p.12** t © Simon Ross, c Paula Bronstein/Getty Images; **p.16** t © Noah Addis/Corbis, b © Stockbyte/Photolibrary Group Ltd; **p.17** Ian West/PA Archive/Press Association Images; **p.19** DAVID GUTTENFELDER/AP/Press Association Images; **p.21** DESMOND KWANDE/AFP/Getty Images; **p.27** ©Nick Middleton; **p.29** NASA image courtesy Jeff Schmaltz, MODIS Land Rapid Response Team at NASA GSFC; **p.30** Lieut. Commander Mark Moran, NOAA Corps, NMAO/AOC; **p.31** AFP/Getty Images; **p.33** Steven Kazlowski/photolibrary.com; **p.34** tr Daniel Beltra/Archivo Museo Salesiano/Greenpeace, br KATSUMI KASAHARA/AP/Press Association Images; **p.36** tr JEROME FAVRE/AP/Press Association Images, bl © Stockbyte/Photolibrary Group Ltd; **p.37** © Broudy/Donohue Photography/Corbis; **p.38** World Ocean Floor Panorama by Bruce C. Heezen and Marie Tharp, 1977. © Marie Tharp 1977/2003. Reproduced by permission of Marie Tharp Maps, LLC 8 Edward Street, Sparkill, New York 10976; **p.40** © Photodisc/Getty Images; **p.43** l © Arctic-Images/Corbis, r © Annette Soumillard/Hemis/Corbis; **p.44** Photo by T. Kobayashi, Univ. Kagoshima. Japan, Nov 5, 1991/U.S.Geological Survey; **p.45** PLANETOBSERVER/SCIENCE PHOTO LIBRARY; **p.46** m © Roger Ressmeyer/Corbis; **p.47** Frederic Dupoux/Getty Images; **p.50** t JOHN RUSSELL/AFP/Getty Images, b SENA VIDANAGAMA/AFP/Getty Images; **p.51** © Altaf Hussain/Reuters/Corbis; **p.53** l © Photodisc/Getty Images, r © Simon Ross, b © Photolibrary Group Ltd; **p.55** © Photodisc/Getty Images; **p.56** © Simon Stirrup/Alamy; **p.57** Victor Englebert/Time Life Pictures/Getty Images; **p.59** © Simon Ross; **p.61** t Tony Escritt, b Alison Wright/Robert Harding/Rex Features; **p.62** © Photolibrary Group Ltd; **p.64** Mohamad Zaid/Rex Features; **p.65** Darrell Gulin/Photographer's Choice/Getty Images; **p.66** © Panorama Media (Beijing) Ltd./Alamy; **p.67** Image Source/Getty Images; **p.70** © Philippe Lissac/Godong/Corbis; **p.73** © Image Source - World Portraits/Alamy; **p.74** © Jacky Naegelen/Reuters/CORBIS; **p.75** © Jacky Naegelen/Reuters/CORBIS; **p.76** AP/Press Association Images; **p.78** tl Elena Segatini/Getty Images, tr Steven L. Raymer/National Geographic/Getty Images, c © Jim Zuckerman/Corbis, b © Image Source/Corbis; **p.79** l Umesh Goswami/The India Today Group/Getty Images, r Swami Stream/Swaminathan/Licensed under the Creative Commons Attribution 2.0 Generic license; **p.80** Rex Features; **p.82** © Atlantide Phototravel/Corbis; **p.84** KARIM SAHIB/AFP/Getty Images; **p.85** © Barbar Walton/epa/Corbis; **p.86** Dan Kitwood/Getty Images; **p.88** © Rick Dalton/AgStock Images/Corbis; **p.89** © Imagestate Media; **p.91** Ruth Lowe; **p.92** Adeel Halim/Bloomberg via Getty Images; **p.93** © Trevor Smithers ARPS/Alamy; **p.94** Simon Rawles; **p.95** l © Art Directors & TRIP/Alamy, r Josef Polleross/Anzenberger/eyevine; **p.96** t Brennan Linsley/AP/Press Association, b © Raymond Gehman/Corbis; **p.97** © Hugues de Latude/Sygma/Corbis; **p.98** © Jon Hrusa/epa/Corbis; **p.99** t © Stockbyte/Photolibrary Group Ltd, b © Photodisc/Getty Images; **p.101** t © Chris Hellier/Corbis, b VYACHESLAV OSELEDKO/AFP/Getty Images; **p.102** Xinhua, Du Huaju/AP/Press Association Images; **p.103** l © Simon Ross, r © Biosphoto/Alcalay Jean-Jacques/Still Pictures; **p.104** © Corbis; **p.108** JOERG BOETHLING/Still Pictures; **p.109** Paul Thompson/Photolibrary.com; **p.110** t © Natalie Fobes/Corbis, b © Mark Conlin/Alamy; **p.111** Adam Butler/AP/Press Association Images; **p.113** t © Jon Hicks/Corbis, cl © Keith Poynton/Alamy, cr © Jon Hicks/Alamy; **p.114** © Aerial Archives/Alamy; **p.115** © Robert Everts/Corbis; **p.116** l © Michele Westmorland/Corbis, r JOJO WALKER/AP/Press Association Images; **p.118** © Erika Antoniazzo/Alamy; **p.119** © REINHARD KRAUSE/Reuters/Corbis; **p.120** Martin Shields/Alamy; **p.121** © Rancho Margot Costa Rica; **p.122** © Frans Lanting/Corbis; **p.123** © Craig Aurness/CORBIS; **p.124** tr © STEVEN SHI/Reuters/Corbis, tl © Yonhap/epa/Corbis, bl NASA Earth Observatory, br Algalita Marine Research Foundation; **p.125** © George Steinmetz/Corbis; **p.126** Herve Gyssels/Photononstop/Photolibrary.com; **p.127** l MARK EDWARDS/Still Pictures, r Melanie Stetson Freeman/The Christian Science Monitor/Getty Images; **p.128** l © Stockbyte/Photolibrary Group Ltd, r © Viviane Moos/Corbis; **p.129** © Kitch Bain - Fotolia.com; **p.130** © RSPB-IMAGES; **p.131** t Algalita Marine Research Foundation, b Algalita Marine Research Foundation; **p.132** © Chris Jordan, Courtesy of Kopeikin Gallery.

Text and image acknowledgements:

p.2 Satellite photograph of the Earth's surface Octopus Publishing Group: *Philip's Modern School Atlas*, © 2007 Philip's; **p.13** Data reproduced by permission of United Nations Development Programme; **p.14** Data reproduced by permission of United Nations Development Programme; **p.27** © Nick Middleton; **p.52** Nusa Factfile Copyright Guardian News & Media Ltd 2005.; **p.57** The Yanomami way of life © Survival International www.survivalinternational.org; **p.58** Amazon Travel Map © ITMB Publishing; **p.68** Egypt Map Extract Octopus Publishing Group: *Philip's Modern School Atlas*, © 2007 Philip's; **p.75** Top countries of origin for refugees © United Nations High Commissioner for Refugees; **p.81** Dubai map extract © Rough Guides part of The Penguin Group; **p.83** Dubai city centre map extract © Rough Guides part of The Penguin Group; **p.97** Extract from the Sudan Tribune © SudanTribune; **p.112** Tourist destination map Octopus Publishing Group: *Philip's Modern School Atlas*, © 2007 Philip's; **p.117** Namibia map extract © ITMB Publishing; **p.130** FSC logo © 1996 Forest Stewardship Council A.C.; **p.130** Deforestation data reproduced by permission of Rhett A. Butler/mongabay.com; **pp.134–137** World maps Octopus Publishing Group: *Philip's Modern School Atlas*, © 2007 Philip's.

Every effort has been made to trace all copyright holders, but if any have been inadvertently overlooked, the Publishers will be pleased to make the necessary arrangements at the first opportunity.

Introduction

A A global sense of place

Look at Figure 1. It is a photograph of the Earth taken from space by a satellite. Look at the landmasses and the huge areas of ocean between them. Can you name any of the landmasses and the oceans? Notice also the clouds in the atmosphere above the Earth's surface.

Environmental groups sometimes use photographs like this one to show that the Earth is isolated in space. If the beauty seen in Figure 1 is to be maintained for the future, we need to look after our planet. We can't simply trash it and move somewhere else!

As geographers, we are mainly interested in the patterns and processes operating on the Earth's surface. We are also interested in some of the processes operating below the surface (such as earthquakes and volcanic activity) and those in the atmosphere above (such as hurricanes). This is because they affect what happens on the Earth's surface. In understanding the world in which we live, geographers will be able to manage and sustain our world for future generations. This is why geography is such an important subject today.

▲ **Figure 1   Earth in space**

Activity

1 Study Figure 2 on the next page. It is a satellite photograph taken from space centred on the Atlantic Ocean. Use the atlas maps at the end of the book to help you answer the following questions.

   a) What is the name of the continent at A?

   b) What is the name of the vast area of tropical rainforest at B?

   c) What is the name of the island at C?

   d) The name of the sea at D is the Caribbean Sea. True or false?

   e) Which is the Red Sea, E or F?

   f) What name is given to the area that is mostly desert at G?

   g) Can you suggest what the white patches are at H? They are not clouds!

   h) Notice that there is a large area of cloud in the north. Use the atlas map to describe how far south this cloud extends over Europe and North America.

   i) Describe the location of cloud over Africa.

   j) The cloud pattern at I is particularly menacing. Do you know what this feature is called?

Areas of vegetation are shown green.

The bright yellow of North Africa is caused by the highly reflective sandy and rocky surface of the Sahara desert.

Cloud patterns can be clearly seen. The brighter the white of the clouds, the thicker they are (the tops of the clouds reflecting sunlight back into space cause this brightness). Thick clouds are likely to bring rain. The small isolated 'blobs' of cloud are isolated shower clouds.

▲ **Figure 2   Satellite photograph of part of Earth's surface**

B Global geography

In a quiz there are often questions about 'geography'. These questions most commonly involve naming locations, such as countries, cities or oceans. It is important for us to have a good knowledge of where places are, before we go on to look at them in detail.

At the end of this book you will find world maps showing physical geography (mountains, rivers, deserts, oceans, etc) and human geography (countries, cities, etc). The following activities will help you to gain a basic knowledge of world geography.

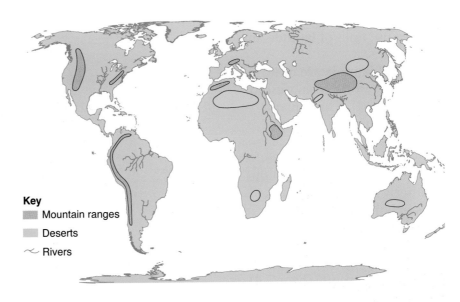

Key
- Mountain ranges
- Deserts
- ∿ Rivers

▲ **Figure 3   Mountain ranges, rivers and deserts of the world**

Activities

2 Study Figure 3. It locates some of the main physical features of the world. These features are shown on the atlas map on pages 134–35.

  a) Make a careful copy of the features shown in Figure 3 on a blank world map. Use colours to shade the mountain ranges, rivers and deserts and explain these colours in a key.

  b) Use the atlas map to write the names of the mountain ranges, rivers and deserts.

  c) Write the names of the following continents in their correct places: Europe, Asia, Africa, Antarctica, North America and South America.

  d) The continent of Oceania covers Australia, New Zealand and the islands of the South Pacific. Add this name to your map.

  e) Now write the names of the following oceans: Pacific, North Atlantic, South Atlantic, Arctic, Southern, Indian.

  f) Add the title 'The world's physical geography'.

3 For this activity you will need a large blank world map. You will need to refer to the atlas map on pages 136–37.

  a) Locate the following cities on your map and label them: New York, Mexico City, Buenos Aires, Rio de Janeiro, London, Moscow, Cairo, Lagos (Nigeria), Tehran, Karachi, Delhi, Beijing, Seoul, Tokyo, Jakarta, Manila.

  b) Locate and label the following countries: Canada, USA, Mexico, Brazil, Argentina, Greenland, Nigeria, Saudi Arabia, Egypt, Iran, Iraq, Russia, India, Pakistan, China, South Korea, Japan, Philippines, Indonesia, Australia, New Zealand.

  c) Choose two or three other cities and countries to locate and label.

  d) Add the title 'World countries and cities'.

4 Carry out a search of recent newspapers or news sites on the internet, such as the BBC, to find information about recent global events (such as floods, earthquakes, sporting events). Try to identify ten to twelve events from around the world. Use the atlas maps to locate these events onto your own A3 world map. Fully label each event and use simple sketches or photos from the internet to illustrate your map. Add the title 'Geography in the news'.

C Latitude and longitude

To locate places on an atlas map we use lines of **latitude** and **longitude**.

Lines of latitude are drawn around the world from west to east (Figure 4). The Equator is the line drawn around the centre of the Earth. This line splits the world into the Northern Hemisphere and the Southern Hemisphere. Other lines of latitude are drawn around the world parallel to the Equator.

Lines of longitude are drawn from north to south (Figure 4). The central line of longitude is called the **Prime Meridian**. It runs through Greenwich in London. Lines of longitude increase both east and west away from the Prime Meridian.

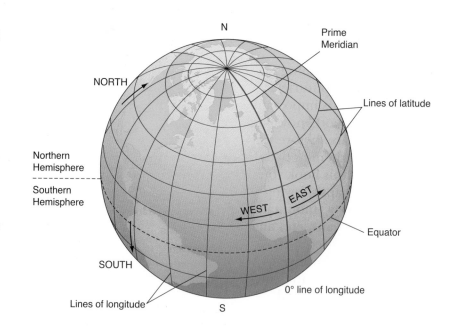

▲ **Figure 4 Lines of latitude and longitude**

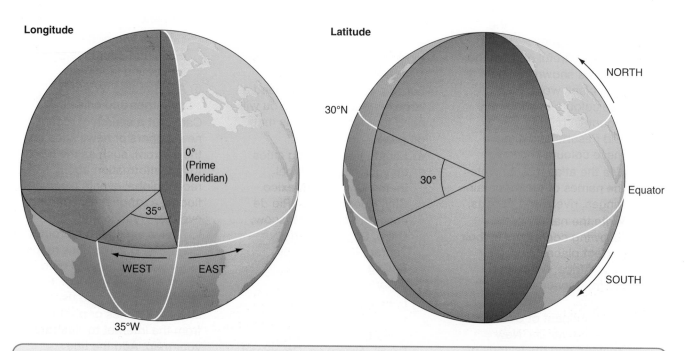

- The values of latitude and longitude are expressed as degrees.
- Lines of latitude extend from 0 degrees at the Equator to 90 degrees at the North Pole and South Pole.
- The lines of longitude increase in both directions away from the Prime Meridian to reach 180 degrees east and west on the opposite side of the Earth.

▲ **Figure 5 How are lines of latitude and longitude drawn using degrees?**

How to find latitude and longitude

On an Ordnance Survey map, each grid line is split into tenths to enable an accurate position to be located by a six-figure grid reference. Degrees of latitude and longitude are also split up. They are split into 60ths referred to as 'minutes'. Look at Figure 6 to see how to locate a place using latitude and longitude.

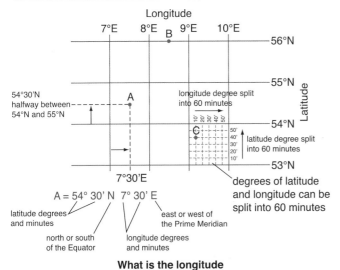

A = 54° 30' N   7° 30' E

latitude degrees and minutes

north or south of the Equator

longitude degrees and minutes

east or west of the Prime Meridian

What is the longitude and latitude of B and C?

▲ **Figure 7   Important lines of latitude and longitude**

◄ **Figure 6   Finding a place using latitude and longitude**

Activities

5 Study Figure 7.

   a) Make a copy of the lines of latitude and longitude on a blank map.

   b) Use the atlas maps in the back of the book to name the following lines that you have drawn:
   - Equator
   - Tropic of Capricorn
   - Tropic of Cancer
   - Antarctic Circle
   - Arctic Circle
   - Prime Meridian

   c) Give your map a title.

6 Study the atlas map on pages 136–37.

   a) Does the Prime Meridian go through Mali or Mauritania?

   b) Which African city is very near the Prime Meridian?

   c) Is Iceland north or south of the Arctic Circle?

   d) Is the Ross Sea north or south of the Antarctic Circle?

   e) The Equator runs through the country of Ecuador. True or false?

   f) Is Hong Kong north or south of the Tropic of Cancer?

   g) Is Perth in Australia north or south of the Tropic of Capricorn?

   h) The Tropic of Capricorn runs through Bolivia. True or false?

   i) Name one African country through which the Equator runs.

   j) Is Malaysia on the Equator?

7 Study the atlas map on pages 134–35. Sort the following mountains, deserts, seas and oceans into those that are north and those that are south of the Equator.

   a) Mountains: Himalayas, Brazilian Highlands, European Alps, Ethiopian Highlands

   b) Deserts: Gobi Desert, Great Victoria Desert (Australia), Kalahari Desert (Africa), Thar Desert (India)

   c) Seas and oceans: Caribbean Sea, Mediterranean Sea, Java Sea (Indonesia), South China Sea

D Time zones

Think back to last March or October. Do you remember that you had to change your clocks and watches? This is due to changes in the hours of daylight as the Earth orbits around the sun. In the summer, we have much longer hours of daylight than in the winter, which is why clocks go forward in March. In October, as the days get shorter, the clocks are put back an hour to give us more daylight at the start of the day, when people are travelling to work or school.

We also have to change our clocks and watches when we travel abroad, especially if we go east or west. To see why, look at Figure 8. It shows the areas of day and night in the world on 5 September 2008 at 11.50am UK time. Some regions of the world are brightly lit up by the sun (day), whereas other parts are in darkness (night).

This is because as the Earth spins on its axis, different areas are exposed to the sun's rays. Remember, the Earth completes one rotation about its axis every 24 hours. On 5 September 2008, the area of daytime (and night!) shown on Figure 8 slowly extended westwards. By 4 pm (UK time), all of USA was enjoying the first hours of daylight. Meanwhile, it was dark in India!

Activity

8 Study Figure 8. You may need to turn to the atlas maps at the end of the book to help you with this activity.

a) Notice that it is daytime in the UK. Which other parts of the world are in daytime?

b) If you were in Sydney, Australia, would it be light or dark?

c) What is the evidence that the Arctic enjoys 24-hours daylight at this time of the year?

d) Can you suggest which part of the world has to cope with 24-hours darkness in December?

e) Describe the differences between the east and west coasts of the USA.

f) By 2.00pm UK time which countries do you think will have become dark since 11.50am UK time?

g) Do you think people in South America will experience longer hours of daylight in December than people in the UK? Why?

▲ **Figure 8 Day–night photograph of the Earth (5 September 2008 11.50am UK time)**

The reason we have to change our clocks and watches when travelling abroad is so that wherever in the world we are, the working day (roughly 9am to 5pm) corresponds with the hours of daylight.

A map of **international time zones** (Figure 9) shows the time differences between places. If we travel west from the UK towards the USA, we have to put our clocks back. If we travel east from the UK towards Eastern Europe and Asia, we have to put our clocks forward. Notice that the pattern of time zones is not equal across the world. This is because individual countries often wish to have a single time zone. China is a good example of this.

Long distance travel (involving crossing several time zones) can affect our natural body clocks, giving us 'jet lag'. It can take a few days for our bodies to get used to living in a different time zone.

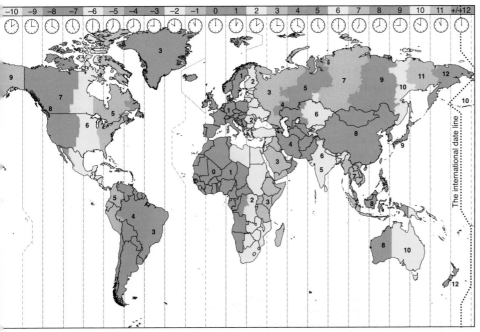

Key

6 Hours behind or ahead of Greenwich Mean Time

—— International boundaries

- - - Time zone boundaries

▲ **Figure 9 Time zones**

Destination	Time difference from London	Departure time (local time)	Arrival time (local time)	Duration of flight
Moscow, Russia	+3 hr	09.30	16.20	3hr 50m
Montreal, Canada		15.00		7hr 35m
Nairobi, Kenya		10.05	21.35	
Hong Kong, China		11.30		11hr 35m
Dallas, USA			15.00	10hr 15m
Delhi, India		20.50	10.40	

▲ **Figure 10 Flight details from London, UK**

Activities

9 Study Figure 9.

a) It is 12 noon in the UK. You receive a telephone call from your aunt in New York. What is her local time?

b) Your older brother is taking a GAP year in Perth, Australia. You have arranged to ring him when he returns from work at 4pm. What time in the UK will you need to call him?

c) You are in Atlanta, USA. It is 9am in the morning. What time is it in Anchorage, Alaska?

d) Why might you be annoyed to receive a phone call from a friend ringing from Hong Kong at 10am local time?

e) What happens if you cross the international date line from Russia into Alaska, USA?

10 Study Figures 9 and 10.

a) Make a copy of Figure 10.

b) Use the time zone map (Figure 9) to work out the **time differences** between London and each destination given in the table. Use a + or – to indicate whether it is ahead or back in time.

c) Now try to complete the missing spaces in Figure 9 using the other details to help you. This is quite difficult so be careful and double-check your working.

E Sustainable development

In geography today, the idea of **sustainable development** is very important. This means improving people's quality of life without causing any long-term harm to the environment.

Look at Figure 11. It shows commercial logging of tropical rainforest in Borneo, Malaysia. Logging here has involved the complete removal of all trees over vast areas of land, an operation called **clearfelling**. When this happens all trees of whatever age are felled. Habitats are totally destroyed, endangering species such as the orang-utan.

A further problem with clearfelling is that it exposes the topsoil to wind and rain, often leading to severe soil erosion. This is an excellent example of unsustainable development. Trees are wiped out and not replaced, habitats are destroyed, species are under threat and soils are damaged.

Today, people realise that we cannot continue to damage the environment. We have to work within environmental limits if future generations are going to be able to benefit from the Earth's resources as we have done. This is at the heart of sustainable development. Throughout this book you will learn about examples of sustainable development.

Activities

11 Study Figure 11. You are a reporter for a national newspaper. Your editor has just received this photograph and wants to use it on the front page of the newspaper as the lead story. You have been asked to write a couple of paragraphs to go alongside the photograph, highlighting some of the issues of deforestation and unsustainable development. You also need to come up with a punchy headline.

12 Study Figure 11. What do you think could be done to reduce the long-term harmful impacts of deforestation on the environment and make logging more sustainable?

▲ **Figure 11   Clearfelling in Borneo**

F Globalisation

In just a few hours, it is possible to fly almost anywhere in the world. Get out of the aeroplane and you will probably see familiar brands of food and drink all around you. McDonald's and KFC will be selling much the same food that you can buy in the UK, billboards will be advertising the latest PlayStation games, cinema blockbusters or mobile phones (Figure 12). Local people may well be wearing clothes similar to yours, using the same brands of soap and shampoo and listening to the same music. This global spread of ideas, products, culture, fashion, foods and drinks is called **globalisation**.

In recent years, it is probably the internet more than anything that has been responsible for globalisation. In a matter of seconds we can send messages or order products from all over the world. Blogging and Twitter are good examples of how information is being spread around the world in an instant. People use the phrase 'the world is getting smaller' to describe the effects of globalisation.

Activity

13 Work as a class to produce a wall display illustrating globalisation. To do this you need to collect information in the form of materials (photographs, food wrappers, magazine adverts, etc.) that illustrate the worldwide spread of materials and ideas. See if you can find evidence (similar to that shown in Figure 12) for American brand names in Russia or Japanese products in the Middle East.

▲ **Figure 12   Globalisation, Novosibirsk, Russia**

G Issue: Why are Wimbledon's tennis balls made in the Philippines?

The Wimbledon tennis championship is one of the sporting highlights of summer in the UK (Figure 13). Over 500 players are involved in the two-week tournament during which some 48,000 Dunlop Slazenger tennis balls are served, volleyed and smashed. Up until recently the tennis balls were manufactured in Barnsley but since 2003 production has moved to the Philippines. Why?

Have you ever looked closely at a tennis ball that has been cut apart? It is essentially a hollow rubber ball covered with a green-yellow wool cloth (Figure 14). It looks quite simple, but is in fact a highly complex scientific-based product that has to have a very precise weight, bounce and texture. Every ball has to be identical. The tins that store the balls are pressurised to retain the bounce and stop the balls going soft. There is a lot more to the humble tennis ball than you might imagine!

Tennis balls demonstrate very clearly the idea of globalisation (Figure 15). Manufactured in the Philippines, the tennis balls are made from materials shipped in from all over the world. A large number of chemicals are imported from all over the world to process the raw rubber that comes from Malaysia. Scientists and sports specialists based outside the Philippines provide technical support to ensure that the tennis balls perform correctly on court. The flows and transfers of materials and ideas across the world demonstrate clearly what globalisation is all about.

▲ Figure 14 Tennis ball

▲ Figure 13 Wimbledon tennis championships

Activity

14 Part A

Draw a large map based on the information contained in Figure 15 to show the global nature of tennis ball production. This will help you to understand what is needed to make tennis balls and will give you some clues to explain why they are made in the Philippines.

Follow the steps below to complete your map.

- On a blank world map plot the global locations shown on Figure 15. Notice that each one is explained in the key.
- Using a pencil first, draw flowlines to show the movement of goods and ideas across the map. Most of your flowlines will go to the Dunlop Slazenger factory in Bataan, Philippines.
- Add a flowline to show how the tennis balls from the Philippines are exported to the UK.
- Now colour the flowlines and explain each of them in a key or by writing a label alongside each line, using the text in the key to Figure 15.
- Use the internet (a good example of globalisation in practice!) to find some photos to illustrate your map.

Key

1   Dunlop Slazenger factory in Bataan, Philippines where the tennis balls are manufactured
2   Wool from sheep in New Zealand is shipped to the UK to be made into the familiar tennis ball green-yellow cloth. It is then shipped to the factory at Bataan
3   Rubber from Malaysia is the main raw material for making the tennis balls at the Bataan factory
4   Zinc oxide is transported to Bataan from Thailand
5   Sulphur is transported to Bataan from South Korea
6   Magnesium carbonate is transported to Bataan from Japan
7   Silica is transported to Bataan from Greece
8   Clay from South Carolina, USA is exported to Bataan
9   Apart from the manufactured wool cloth made in the UK, scientists from UK universities are involved in technical and scientific aspects of the manufacturing process
10 Glue is imported from the southern Philippines
11 Tins are imported from Indonesia

▲ **Figure 15   Global locations involved in making tennis balls**

Activity

14 Part B

Now work in pairs or small groups to discuss the following questions:

a) Why do you think Dunlop Slazenger make tennis balls in the Philippines?

b) Why do you think they moved their factory from Barnsley in the UK to the Philippines?

c) What do you think the impact of the closure of the factory at Barnsley has had on the local community?

d) What do you think has been the impact of establishing a large factory in the Philippines?

e) Do you think that it is a good idea for Wimbledon's tennis balls to be made in the Philippines? Explain your answer.

Development Issues

1

A What is development?

In geography, 'development' means improving people's quality of life. Look at Figure 1. It is a photograph of a group of Year 9 pupils from the UK enjoying a field trip in Chatel, France. They have a pretty good quality of life. They have warm and comfortable homes, enough to eat and drink, a caring family, a good education and plenty of opportunities to look forward to in the future. They can express their opinions freely and, when they are older, will be able to vote in elections.

Now look at the children in Figure 2. Whilst they might be having fun, they are in fact playing in a canal polluted by raw sewage. These children have a relatively poor quality of life. They have a restricted diet, limited access to safe water or sanitation, poor health care, little education and few prospects of secure well-paid employment in the future. Despite the smiles, life for them and their families is very tough indeed.

In this chapter we will examine some aspects of development and we will consider some ways in which the quality of people's lives can be improved.

▲ **Figure 1   Year 9 pupils on a field trip to Chatel, eating chocolate crêpes in a cafe**

▶ **Figure 2 Children playing in a polluted canal in the Philippines**

Activities

1 Study Figure 1.

   a) Work with a friend to make a list of the things that provide you with a good quality of life.

   b) Now discuss your list and select the five most important things that affect your quality of life.

   c) How could your quality of life be improved further?

2 Study Figure 2. By referring only to what you can see in Figure 2, suggest ways that the children's quality of life could be improved.

3 A high level of development does not always bring happiness and satisfaction. In some UK schools, there are even lessons in 'happiness'

because there are concerns about depressed teenagers turning to drugs and alcohol or behaving anti-socially.

   a) Work with a friend to discuss why 'development' does not always bring happiness.

   b) Imagine that your school was to introduce happiness classes for Year 9. What sort of things do you think should be discussed in these lessons? How can teenagers today become happier?

   c) Charities often report that poorer people are more generous than wealthy people. Why do you think this is?

B Can development be measured?

Measuring people's quality of life is virtually impossible. We are all individuals and have different needs and levels of satisfaction. Despite the difficulties in measuring development at an individual level, it is possible to make comparisons between countries.

The best-known and most widely used measure of development is the United Nation's **Human Development Index** (HDI). This brings together four sets of data (see Figure 3) to form a single index number (Figure 4). The calculations involved are complex but the results enable countries to be compared across a range of development indicators. In theory, the higher the Human Development Index the greater the level of development.

Life expectancy at birth – high life expectancy reflects good health care and high standards of living

Adult literacy rate – the percentage of people over fifteen who can read and write. This is a good measure of education

Enrolment rate – a measure of the number of students enrolled in education

Average income – reflects the wealth of the people in a country

▲ **Figure 3 The UN Human Development Index indicators**

Activities

4 Study Figure 3. These four indicators of development are used to calculate the United Nation's HDI.

  a) What is 'adult literacy rate'? Do you think it is a good measure of development? Explain your answer.

  b) Why do you think 'life expectancy' varies between different countries?

5 Study Figure 4, which shows the top, and bottom ten countries based on HDI values.

  a) How many countries in the top ten are European?

  b) Are there any countries missing that you would have expected to be in the top ten? Give reasons for your answer.

  c) How many countries in the bottom ten are in Africa?

  d) Do you think it is fair to state that Africa appears to be the least developed continent in the world? Explain your answer.

  e) Calculate the difference in the HDI between the 1st and the 10th ranked countries. Now do the same between the 168th and 177th countries. What do you notice about the spread of values?

Ranking (out of 177)	Country	HDI
1	Iceland	0.968
2	Norway	0.968
3	Australia	0.962
4	Canada	0.961
5	Ireland	0.959
6	Sweden	0.956
7	Switzerland	0.955
8	Japan	0.953
9	Netherlands	0.953
10	France	0.952

▲ **Figure 4a Top ten countries according to the HDI (2005)**

Ranking (out of 177)	Country	HDI
168	Dem. Rep. Congo	0.411
169	Ethiopia	0.406
170	Chad	0.388
171	Central African Republic	0.384
172	Mozambique	0.384
173	Mali	0.380
174	Niger	0.374
175	Guinea-Bissau	0.374
176	Burkina Faso	0.370
177	Sierra Leone	0.336

▲ **Figure 4b Bottom ten countries according to the HDI (2005)**

Country	HDI	Ranked position for HDI	GDP (per person $US)	Ranked position for GDP
Iceland	0.968	1	36,510	2
Japan	0.953	2	31,267	
USA	0.951	3	41,890	1
UK	0.946	4	33,328	3
Singapore	0.922	5	29,663	
Mexico	0.829	6	10,751	
Russian Federation	0.802	7	10,845	
China	0.777	8	6,757	
Jamaica	0.736	9	4,291	
Botswana	0.654	10	12,387	
Bangladesh	0.547	11	2,053	
Zimbabwe	0.513	12	2,038	
Nigeria	0.470	13	1,128	
Ethiopia	0.406	14	1,055	
Sierra Leone	0.336	15	806	

GDP = Gross Domestic Product (a measure of the wealth of a country)

▲ **Figure 5   HDI and GDP rankings**

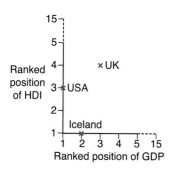

▲ **Figure 6   Scattergraph showing the relationship between GDP and HDI**

Activity

6   Study Figure 5. In this activity you are going to draw a **scattergraph** to see if there is a relationship between the overall HDI of a country and its wealth, as measured by GDP. In theory, it is reasonable to expect that the wealthier a country, the higher its level of development. This is because the country can afford good health care and schools and has a plentiful supply of food. Let's see if this is true!

a)   Copy Figure 5 and complete the final column giving the ranked position of each country according to its GDP. The first three rankings have been done for you.

b)   Make a copy of Figure 6 on a sheet of graph paper.

c)   Plot the values for the 15 countries. Notice that three of them have been done for you. Use a key to identify each country. Your completed graph with a 'scatter' of points is called a scattergraph.

d)   Draw a best-fit line to show the general trend of the points (see Figure 7). The best-fit line should aim to run through the centre of the points. It does not have to run through the origin of the graph.

e)   Now discuss the results using Figure 7 to help you.

f)   Does there appear to be a relationship between GDP and HDI? Is it what we expected?

g)   Are there any anomalies?

h)   Carry out some research on the Internet to see if you can explain any anomalies that you have identified.

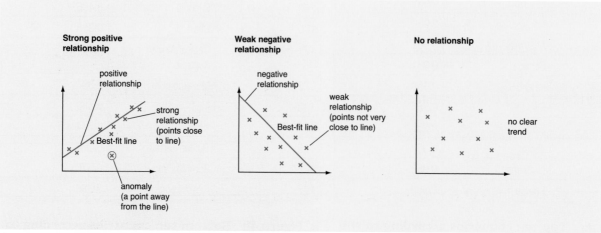

▲ **Figure 7   How to interpret a scattergraph**

C Patterns of development: rich world, poor world?

Look at Figure 8. It shows the Human Development Index (HDI) values plotted on a world map. This detailed map is produced by the United Nations. Notice in the key that the HDI values have been separated into high, medium and low levels of development.

The countries with the highest levels of development include much of Western Europe, North America and Oceania (Australia and New Zealand). This supports the data in Figure 4a (page 13) that shows the top ten countries. Look at the bottom ten countries in Figure 4b. They are all in Africa. Now look at Figure 8 to see if Africa is indeed the continent with the lowest levels of development.

Having drawn the scattergraph in Activity 6, you have identified a close relationship between the levels of development as measured by the HDI and the wealth of a country as measured by GDP. Therefore, it could be suggested that the map in Figure 8 not only shows levels of development but it gives us a good idea of relative wealth too. Do you agree with this assumption?

Activity

7 Study Figure 8. Use the atlas map on pages 136–37 to help you with this activity.

a) Name one country outside Africa that has a low level of development.

b) Which country has the highest level of development in South America?

c) Which African countries have the highest level of development?

d) Does Mexico have a high, medium or low level of development?

e) Does India have a high, medium or low level of development?

f) In what ways do you think this map might be different in five years' time? Give reasons for your answer.

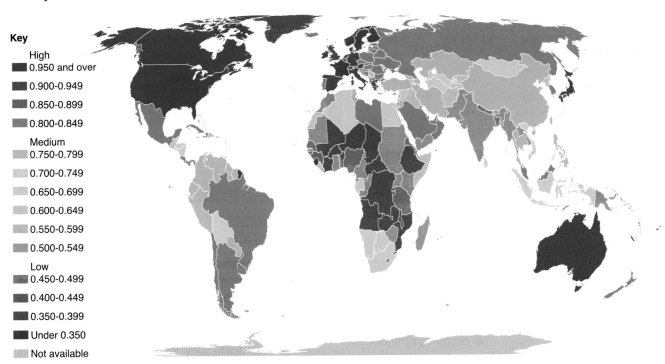

Key

High
- 0.950 and over
- 0.900-0.949
- 0.850-0.899
- 0.800-0.849

Medium
- 0.750-0.799
- 0.700-0.749
- 0.650-0.699
- 0.600-0.649
- 0.550-0.599
- 0.500-0.549

Low
- 0.450-0.499
- 0.400-0.449
- 0.350-0.399
- Under 0.350
- Not available

▲ **Figure 8   Global pattern of the Human Development Index (2007)**

Within every country there are huge variations in levels of development. Look at Figure 9, which shows part of the Brazilian city of Sao Paulo. Brazil has an HDI value of 0.800 placing it in the 'high' development category in Figure 8 (page 15). Just one photograph in one city can show great contrasts in people's quality of life. Imagine how the contrasts are even more extreme between Brazilian city dwellers and those living deep in the heart of the Amazon rainforest.

Activity

8 Study Figure 9.

 a) Describe the different levels of development shown in the photograph.

 b) Do you think the single HDI value for the whole of Brazil is misleading?

 c) Can you think of examples in the UK where there are large variations in levels of development and quality of life?

▲ **Figure 9 Contrasts in development and quality of life in Sao Paulo, Brazil**

D Living off rubbish: the poverty trap

Thirty-five miles to the north of Lima (the capital of Peru), the rubbish of nine million people is dumped in a huge valley. Despite the horrendous smell, the rats and the wild dogs, this rubbish dump is home to a community who live off the rubbish (Figure 10). Many of these people who earn a meagre living by sifting through other people's rotting waste and then re-selling it are children. These children earn money to support themselves and their families. They are often unable to attend school regularly. Caught in a poverty trap without education, they are unlikely to improve the quality of their lives in the future.

▶ **Figure 10 Living and working in Lima's 'rubbish city'**

Diego's story

Diego is a 14-year-old boy who lives in a rundown town on the outskirts of Lima. He is one of many children who work the filthy streets on a rubbish truck, collecting and sorting litter and waste from outside houses.

It is a dangerous and disgusting job that earns him the equivalent of £2 for 10 hours' work. Since his father died, Diego and his four brothers have all had to work to support the family. Diego works alternate days so that he can at least attend school every other day.

Apart from the many scars on his hands, caused by cuts from rusty cans and broken glass, Diego has a terrible cough brought on by the many germs present in the stinking, rotting rubbish. He has to be careful not to be hit by the other rubbish trucks that speed along the city's roads.

Diego is one of many children in Lima, and throughout the world, who are involved in child labour. When faced with extreme poverty, families have to rely on children to earn money, often by doing dangerous and poorly paid jobs.

Activity

9 Study Figure 10.

   a) Describe the clothes worn by the young child. What does this tell you about the poverty of life here?

   b) What do you think the man in the background is doing?

   c) Describe the types of rubbish in this open dump.

   d) Why is this a dangerous place to live and work?

   e) Close your eyes and try to imagine what it is like living on the rubbish dump. Describe the likely sounds and smells.

   f) Should people be allowed to live and scavenge on rubbish dumps?

   g) What could be done to help people who feel the need to work on rubbish dumps?

Helping Peru's child workers: Sport Relief and Bruce Peru

Have you heard of the charity Sport Relief? Each year thousands of people take part in sporting events such as 'fun runs' throughout the UK to raise money for this charity (Figure 11). Some of the money raised has been used to support the work of local Peruvian children's charities to fund local schools in deprived areas, by providing additional staff and resources (such as computers). Many children who used to work on the city's rubbish heaps are now able to attend school. Sport Relief has also provided medical help and food. Liana is a 13-year-old girl who now regularly attends school having spent years making bricks in a dusty quarry. For the first time in her life she has something to look forward to. She is ambitious and wants to be a lawyer.

▲ Figure II Sport Relief charity event

Another charity, Bruce Peru, also supports children by providing food, clothing and educational opportunities. Volunteers based in the areas where the children live help to raise their educational standards to enable them to enter mainstream schooling. To do this they often set up their own schools. Education is seen as the long-term future for improving people's quality of life.

For the first time, these children have the opportunity to attend nearby schools that are well equipped and offer real hope for the future.

Activity

10 For this activity you need to work in pairs or small groups. The aim of the activity is to design a school curriculum aimed at 13- to 14-year-olds who have spent most of their early years working on a rubbish dump. In deciding on your curriculum you need to be aware of the following details about the school:

- The school day runs from 8am to 1pm.
- There are two classrooms for 13- to 14-year-olds, each able to accommodate up to 30 children. There are four other classrooms.
- There is electricity and each classroom has a computer. However, internet access is unreliable.
- Each classroom has chairs and tables and a blackboard.
- There is paper and pencils and a few old textbooks.

- There is a small kitchen with running water.
- There is an area of open ground for children to play.

a) Plan a curriculum for the 13- to 14-year-olds for the week (Monday to Friday). Think about what these children should be taught. What skills are most important for them to learn to provide them with opportunities to improve the quality of their lives in the future? Try not to think about just the traditional subjects taught in the UK.

b) Imagine that a charity has offered to provide support materials. What materials do you think would be most useful and why?

c) Discuss your ideas with the rest of your class.

E Aid and development

Aid is all about providing support for people living in poverty or facing hardship. Take a look in any newspaper and you will see requests for money from a range of organisations, usually charities such as Oxfam, Action Aid or CAFOD. Whilst most appeals are for people living in the poorer regions of the world, support is also requested for disadvantaged members of society in the UK and elsewhere.

Disaster relief

Appeals for money often follow natural disasters such as floods and earthquakes, or outbreaks of disease. Displaced people, forced to flee war-torn regions, often end up in refugee camps where they suffer shortages of food, water and medical support (Figure 12). These demands for support are examples of **emergency aid**. The people affected need support immediately. Whilst this type of aid is important under certain circumstances, it does not address the long-term

issues faced by people in the impoverished parts of the world.

Long-term aid

Long-term aid involves helping people to help themselves. There is a well-known proverb:

'Give a man a fish; you have fed him for today. Teach a man to fish; and you have fed him for a lifetime.'

Author unknown

Whilst it is often necessary to provide food, water and shelter during an emergency, such donations do not help people in the long run. For example, providing supplies of cheap food undercuts the food produced by local farmers. They would risk going out of business if cheap food continued to flood the market. This would lead to a reduction in the amount of food produced locally in the future.

Long-term aid is often received from international organisations (such as the United Nations and the European Union). It can also be donated unilaterally from one country to another, for example, the UK government may decide to support projects in India. Other major suppliers of aid are **non-governmental organisations** (NGOs), in particular, the charities.

You have already come across the work of Sport Relief in Peru. Their support of local charities is an excellent example of long-term aid where the emphasis is placed upon educating children for the future. You will come across several other examples of both emergency and long-term aid elsewhere in this book.

▲ **Figure 12   Refugee camp**

Activities

11 Study Figure 12. For this activity you need to work in pairs or small groups.

   a) Suggest, using evidence from the photograph, the immediate (emergency) needs of the people shown in the photograph.

   b) Make a list of the items that you think should be sent to support the people.

   c) Suggest the long-term needs of the people.

   d) How do you think these long-term needs could be satisfied?

12 Read the fable in Figure 13 (page 20). A fable is a story that attempts to make a serious point. You may need to read it more than once and discuss it as a class before attempting the following activity.

   a) Who do you think are the 'Experts'?

   b) What was the purpose of encouraging a local villager to buy a motorbike?

   c) Do you think the village elders (the 'greybeards') were right to warn the young men?

   d) How did the capital city benefit from the changes in the village?

   e) How did the Maharaja benefit?

   f) Do you think the local people benefited? Explain your answer.

   g) What is the serious point being made by this fable?

   h) Make up your own version of this fable based on farmers growing fruit or vegetables. First make up a story and then create a storyboard rather like Figure 13 to tell your story.

1 The Experts arrived at the fishing village. For years the natives had used primitive techniques in their work. True, they caught fish, but they had to paddle out to sea every day, even on feast days. It was a hard life, though well tried over the years.

2 The new nets were rather dearer than the old and the method of fishing was different too. But in a single net they caught a whole week's supply. Fantastic! You could work one day and be free for the rest of the week! The village folk had a great feast, several feasts ... in fact so many that they had to fish two days a week to pay for all the celebrations.

3 This is no good, thought the Experts, they should be fishing six days a week and making money out of it. We haven't come here to witness endless parties. Surely it's enough with one feast a month. This is an underdeveloped country, they must produce more protein. Fish!

But the village folk favoured fiesta. Fishing two days and free the rest of the week.

4 The Experts grew annoyed. They hadn't travelled from the distant North to watch the natives drum, dance and dream. They had come to fill empty stomachs to lessen the threat of the undernourished against the overfed.

Yet the villagers danced late into the night. Why shouldn't they? They were rich now, almost as rich as the Maharaja, though he had never done a day's work in his life ...

5 And then the Project Director had a brilliant idea. (Not for nothing had he taken an evening course back home in economics.) These lazy fisherfolk were not actually lazy: they were simply weak on motivation, motivation to work harder. They had not discovered their needs.

6 He bribed a villager to buy a motorbike. Bribery was distasteful but sometimes necessary. True, there were roads as such, but the wet sand along the water's edge was hard and smooth.

9 But, probably the most pleased of all was the Maharaja, for it so happens that he was sole agent for the motorcycle firm in that country. He also owned the main fish market in the city, while his uncle's family owned and ran the fishmeal factory. When the experts flew home he raised the price of a motorcycle, so that to buy one, a man must work three years instead of a single season.

And the fishermen fished on. They had discovered a 'need'!

7 The motorcycle roared back and forth. What a toy! And soon every young man wanted one of his own. The village elder warned them: 'What use is there in riding back and forth on the sand?'

But the young men replied: 'We can race. We shall see who is the fastest. And you greybeards, you can place bets on us.'

8 The Project Director's idea proved a brilliant success. At last the men fished almost every day. The capital city got the fresh fish it needed (indeed, a large part is now turned into fishmeal and exported to Europe where it makes excellent pig food and helps keep down the price of bacon!).

▲ **Figure 13   A fable questioning 'development'**

F Issue: How can the threat of cholera be reduced?

In 2008, Zimbabwe was hit by a serious outbreak of cholera (Figure 14). In a country facing a desperate economic and political situation, basic services collapsed. In the capital Harare, rainwater soaked through rubbish and washed raw sewage into rivers and reservoirs. The same water leached through the soil and into the underground boreholes from where people obtain their drinking water. Recently buried bodies in shallow graves further contaminated the water. Several thousand people died from this outbreak of cholera.

What is cholera?

Cholera is an intestinal disease caused by a bacterium found in water contaminated by the human waste of an infected person. It causes severe diarrhoea and vomiting. If it is not treated, it can lead to dehydration and death. The very young and elderly are particularly vulnerable. The disease spreads very quickly where there is poor sanitation and a lack of safe fresh water. In parts of Zimbabwe, the sanitation system stopped working in 2002 and fresh water supplies have become polluted as sewage pipes have ruptured.

Whilst cholera is most frequently reported in poorer parts of the world, particularly in Africa, outbreaks can occur almost anywhere. In 2007, cholera was reported in many countries across the world including the UK and the USA (Figure 15, page 22).

How can cholera be treated?

Cholera can be treated relatively simply and cheaply, through the use of fresh water and rehydration salts. With medical support people infected by cholera can be treated successfully.

Cholera is a preventable disease. In the long term, the provision of effective sanitation and fresh water systems is essential. Flush toilets connected to an efficient sewage system should prevent sewage contaminating fresh water supplies. People in rural areas need to avoid using '**bush toilets**', which can lead to faecal infections being passed into rivers.

 ICT ACTIVITY

Use the internet to find out more about the cholera outbreak that struck Zimbabwe in 2008.
- Did it affect both urban and rural areas?
- What were the main causes?
- How many people died?
- What has been done to treat the infected and prevent the spread of the disease?

◀ **Figure 14   Dirty water flowing through the street in Zimbabwe, 2008**

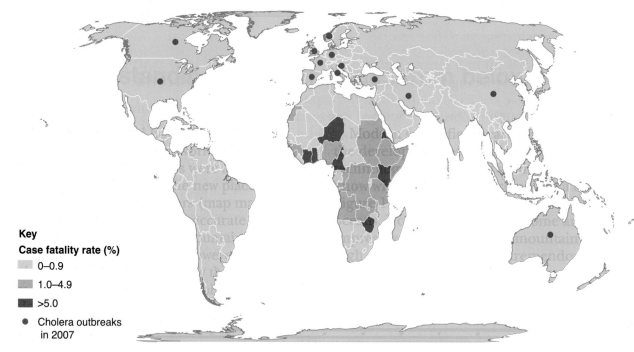

Key
Case fatality rate (%)
- 0–0.9
- 1.0–4.9
- >5.0
- Cholera outbreaks
  in 2007

▲ **Figure 15   Global cholera outbreak, 2007**

The spread of cholera can also be reduced by a number of simple practices, such as washing hands after going to the toilet, eating hot food that has been cooked thoroughly, and not eating the skin of fruit and vegetables that may have been washed in dirty water. Look at Figure 16, which offered advice to New Yorkers facing a cholera outbreak in the 1830s.

▲ **Figure 16**

Activity

13 People living in a small village in a remote part of rural Zimbabwe have been affected by cholera. Several people have died and many others have been infected. Until recently the sanitation system was broken, but it is now working again. Drinking water comes from a deep well and this is safe to drink. However, the cholera bacteria may still contaminate other water sources such as ponds, streams and rivers.

You work for an international charity. You have been asked to produce an information board to inform people how to reduce the risk of a further cholera outbreak in the area. In effect, you are aiming to produce an up-to-date version of Figure 16! Your information board, which will be located in a village community health centre, should include some simple illustrations to support brief written instructions. Most people speak some English, but only at a basic level. This activity can be done individually or in pairs.

Further information on the prevention of cholera can be found on the World Health Organisation's website at **www.who.int/topics/cholera/en**.

Weather and Climate

2

A Global weather

Do you remember the difference between 'weather' and 'climate'? The weather describes the day-to-day conditions of the atmosphere, whereas the climate describes the average weather recorded over a period of 30 years.

Look at Figure 1. It is a map that describes the weather experienced around the world at 12 noon (GMT) on 31 December 2008. Notice that there are considerable differences in the weather experienced around the world. In the UK it was a very cold and frosty New Year's Eve, and people had to wrap up warmly as they celebrated the New Year with various outdoor events. In contrast, people celebrating New Year in New Zealand and Australia were able to do so in shorts and T-shirts!

One of the main factors affecting the global weather is the seasons. December is winter in the Northern Hemisphere and the sun is low in the sky. This explains the low temperatures in Northern Europe, the USA and parts of China. For people living in the Southern Hemisphere, December is summer with a powerful sun high in the sky. Look at the temperatures in South America and South Asia to see how they are much higher than in the Northern Hemisphere.

Another important factor affecting the weather in Figure 1 is night and day (see Figure 8, page 6). At 12 noon (GMT) it is night-time across much of Asia, Australia, New Zealand and the western side of North America.

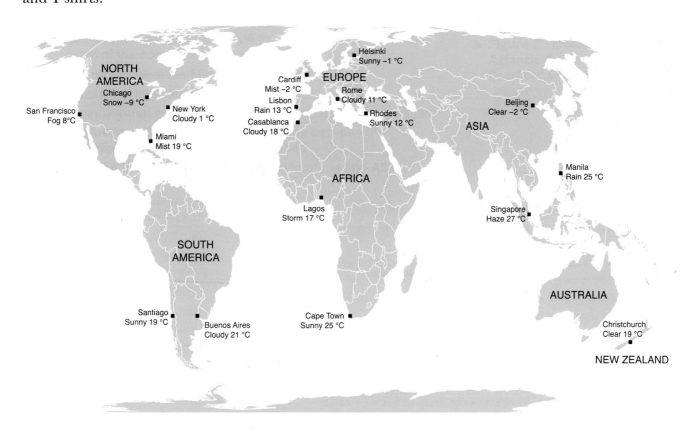

▲ **Figure 1 Global weather 31 December 2008 (12 noon GMT)**

23

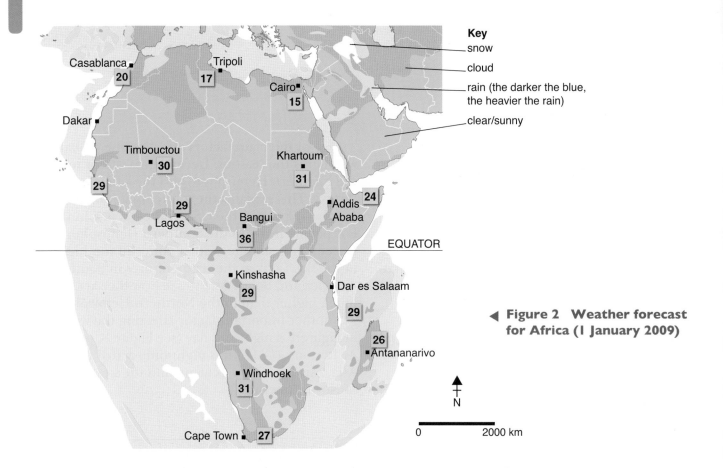

Key
snow
cloud
rain (the darker the blue, the heavier the rain)
clear/sunny

◄ **Figure 2   Weather forecast for Africa (1 January 2009)**

 ICT ACTIVITY

- Use the internet to construct a map similar to Figure 1 to describe the current world weather. Access the Met Office website at
  www.metoffice.gov.uk/weather/world/world_latest.html and record the current weather for a number of selected locations around the world. Make up your own weather symbols to make your map more interesting.
- Weather forecasts similar to that in Figure 2 can be accessed at the BBC's website at www.bbc.co.uk/weather/world.
  - Select a region of the world of your choice, e.g. Africa.
  - Now copy and paste the image of your chosen region into a Word® document. Use text boxes to add labels to describe the weather at each of the locations (alternatively, print the map and add the weather details by hand).
  - Write a weather forecast in the style of a TV or radio weather forecast presentation.
  - Present your forecast 'live' to the rest of the class!
  - Click one of the cities shown (notice that this gives you weather details for your chosen location).

Activity

1. Study Figure 2. It is a weather forecast for Africa for 1 January 2009. Use the atlas map on pages 136–37 to help you with the following questions.

   a) Describe the weather forecast for the following places:
      - Cairo
      - Timbouctou
      - Kinshasha
      - Cape Town

   b) Describe the pattern of rainfall in Africa.

   c) Where is the heaviest rain predicted to fall?

   d) Where is the highest temperature expected and what is it?

   e) How can seasonal differences help to account for the much lower temperatures in the north of Africa?

B Global climates

Look at Figure 3. It is a map that shows the distribution of the world's major climate zones. These climate zones have been determined by patterns of temperature and rainfall. The main features of these climates are described in Figure 4.

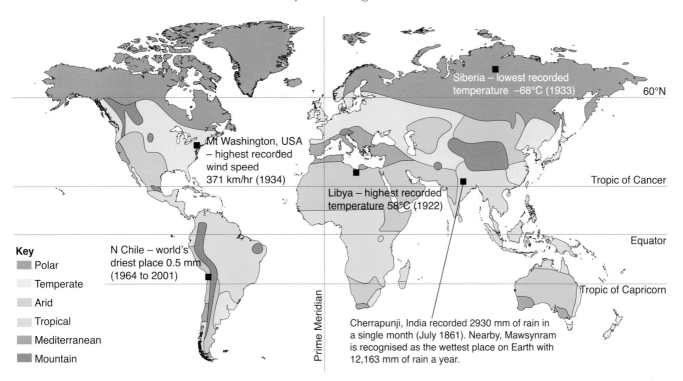

Key
- Polar
- Temperate
- Arid
- Tropical
- Mediterranean
- Mountain

Siberia – lowest recorded temperature –68°C (1933)

Mt Washington, USA – highest recorded wind speed 371 km/hr (1934)

Libya – highest recorded temperature 58°C (1922)

N Chile – world's driest place 0.5 mm (1964 to 2001)

Cherrapunji, India recorded 2930 mm of rain in a single month (July 1861). Nearby, Mawsynram is recognised as the wettest place on Earth with 12,163 mm of rain a year.

60°N

Tropic of Cancer

Equator

Tropic of Capricorn

Prime Meridian

▲ **Figure 3   World climates**

Climate name	Main characteristics	Location
Polar	Very cold and dry throughout the year.	Broad belt stretching across the world mostly north of latitude 60 degrees North. Includes Canada, parts of Scandinavia and Russia.
Temperate	Warm summers and cool winters. Rain throughout the year.	
Arid	Dry with very hot summers and surprisingly cold winters when snow may fall.	
Tropical	Hot and wet throughout the year. Torrential rain and violent storms may occur.	
Mediterranean	Hot dry summers and mild, but often rather wet winters.	
Mountain	Wet throughout the year with snow in the winter. Generally cold throughout the year.	

▲ **Figure 4   World climates table**

Activity

2 Study Figure 3.

a) **Where in the world was the highest temperature recorded?**

b) **What is the name of the desert where this extreme temperature was recorded?**

c) **How many metres of rain fell in Cherrapunji, India in July 1861? Measure this on your classroom wall!**

d) **Cherrapungi and nearby Mawsynram are located just to the south of which major mountain range?**

e) **How do you think the extremely low winter temperatures in Siberia affect people?**

There are three main factors affecting the distribution of the world's climates:

1. **Latitude**. When the sun's rays strike the surface of the Earth the energy warms the surface. At the Equator the sun appears directly overhead and this concentrates the energy, resulting in high temperatures (Figure 5). Away from the Equator towards the Poles, the curvature of the Earth's surface results in the sun appearing to be lower in the sky. The sun's rays are now arriving at a sharper angle and the energy on the surface is more spread out and less effective (Figure 5). This explains why the equatorial climates are warmer than the polar climates.

2. **Continentality**. The nature of the Earth's surface has a big influence on temperature and rainfall. Land warms up and cools down much more quickly than the sea. This explains why large continental regions, such as central Europe and Asia, experience warmer summers and colder winters than coastal regions. Land areas also tend to be drier as they are further away from the influence of the oceans.

3. **Altitude**. If you have walked up a mountain you will know that it tends to get colder the higher up you go. If you go skiing in the winter, you will head for mountains, such as the Alps. Mountains also tend to have more rainfall.

Activity

3 Study Figures 3, 4 and 5 on pages 25 and 26. You may wish to use the atlas maps in the back of the book to help you with this activity.

a) Make a copy of Figure 4.

b) Use Figure 3 and the atlas maps to complete the third column describing the location of each climate zone. Refer to world regions or countries. The location of polar climates has been completed for you.

c) In which climate zone is the Equator found?

d) Look at the parts of the world with a polar climate. What is missing from Figure 3?

e) Use Figure 5 to explain why it is hotter at the Equator than it is at the Poles.

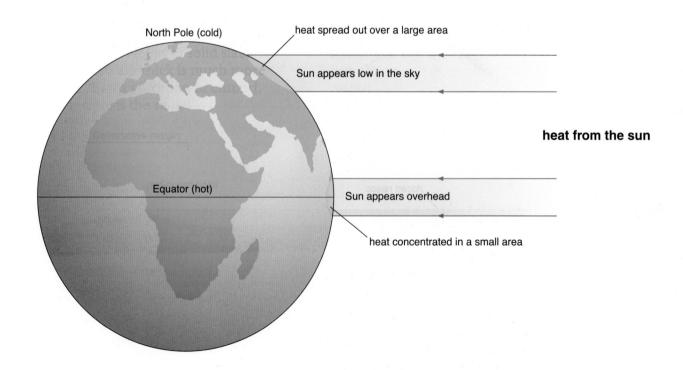

▲ **Figure 5 The effect of latitude on temperature**

C Living in the wettest place on Earth: Mawsynram, India

Look back to Figure 3 on page 25 and locate the wettest place on Earth in northeast India. The towns and villages high in the Meghalaya uplands compete with each other for the title of 'the wettest place on Earth'. Until recently, the 'honour' went to Cherrapunji, where a staggering 22,000 mm of rain fell in a single year in 1861. However, it is now generally accepted that nearby Mawsynram, with an annual rainfall in excess of 12,000 mm is officially the wettest place on Earth. Compare this with London's average annual rainfall of just 600 mm!

Mawsynram lies perched above misty valleys in this remote and inaccessible part of India. From May to September, rain falls almost continuously from dark menacing clouds, drumming loudly on the tin roofs of the houses (Figure 6). Imagine what it must be like to live in such conditions day after day.

Most of the rain actually falls at night so that life during the day is not too disrupted. Indeed, the heavy rainfall ensures that the vegetation in the area is very lush and rich in wildlife. Despite its extreme climate, nearby Cherrapunji is a tourist destination for people interested in nature.

'The rain came down in torrents. The heavens didn't open because you couldn't really see them, but they just sent forth an immense outpouring of water that was truly cosmic in its proportions. It was as if the bottom had fallen out of an ocean in the sky. It rained and it rained and it rained and it rained. It just kept on raining, non-stop for five days, an unremitting, incessant, ear-hurting deluge.'

Nick Middleton, *Going to Extremes*, 2001 Channel 4 Books

▲ **Figure 6   People sheltering from the rain in Mawsynram**

Activity

4 Study Figure 6.

a) How are the people in the photograph protecting themselves from the heavy rain?

b) What are they wearing on their feet? Why are these shoes appropriate given the wet conditions?

c) Imagine that you were standing with the people in the photograph. Do you think it would be noisy? Explain your answer.

d) Can you identify two features of the house that have been specifically designed to cope with the wet climate?

e) Draw a sketch of the building in the photograph. Add labels to describe the building materials used in its construction and the special design features identified in question (d) above.

f) Suggest some everyday problems that you would have to cope with if you had to endure 'incessant' rain like the people who live in Mawsynram.

The extremely heavy rain in this part of India is caused by a seasonal weather event called the **monsoon** (Figure 7). Each year from about May through to September, south-westerly winds carry huge amounts of moisture from the Indian Ocean, bringing heavy rain to India, Bangladesh and parts of Pakistan. As this warm moist air is forced to rise by the Meghalaya uplands it triggers the extreme quantities of rainfall experienced by Cherrapunji and Mawsynram.

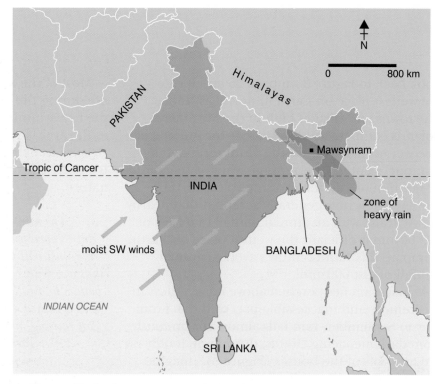

▲ **Figure 7   Indian monsoon (May–September)**

RESEARCH

Carry out your own study of living in an extreme climate. Make a choice between living in the extreme cold of Siberia and the intense dry conditions in northern Chile. Try to discover the following:

- Some facts and figures about the climate in your chosen region
- Why the climate is so extreme
- How the climate affects people's daily lives (try to find a photograph)
- How people have adapted to the climate. For example, see if you can find out about 'water harvesting' in Chile, where local people obtain water from fog!

The following websites will get you started on your research.

- Chile: the driest place on Earth

  www.travelpod.com/travel-blog-entries/ robfrumkin/robworld0607/1174746300/tpod.html

  www.extremescience.com/DriestPlace.htm

- Siberia: the coldest place on Earth

  http://seattletimes.nwsource.com/html/ nationworld/2002189769_cold25.html

  www.youtube.com/watch?v=rZjfScL_wRE (superb video)

D   Extreme weather: hurricanes

Look at Figure 8. It is a satellite photograph of Hurricane Katrina as it approached New Orleans in the USA on 28 August 2005. Visible from space and instantly recognisable with its central '**eye**', this spinning swirl of destruction killed 1,800 people and caused hundreds of billions of dollars worth of damage. It was the most expensive natural disaster in American history.

How do hurricanes form?

Hurricanes (or cyclones) are immensely powerful storms that form over the warm tropical oceans in summer when the water temperature reaches a critical 26.5 °C. Figure 9 shows the main areas of the world where hurricanes form and the common tracks that they take. A hurricane can be up to 10 miles high and 500 miles wide. It moves like a giant spinning top, or Catherine Wheel, at a speed of about 20 mph. As it tracks across the ocean, it picks up warmth and moisture, causing it to grow more powerful and expand in size (Figure 10, page 30). When it hits land it is capable of packing a very powerful punch!

▲ **Figure 8   Satellite image of Hurricane Katrina**

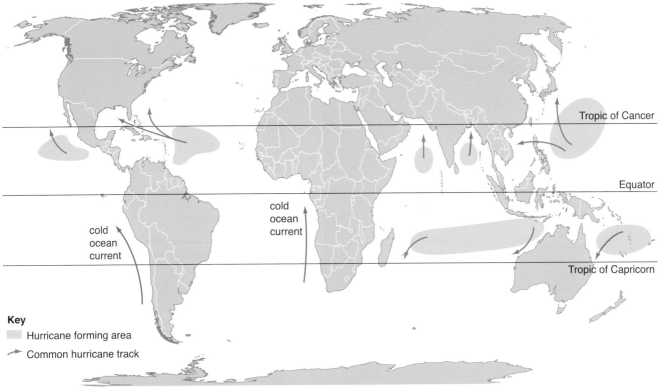

Key

■ Hurricane forming area

↶ Common hurricane track

▲ **Figure 9   Hurricane forming areas**

SUMMER

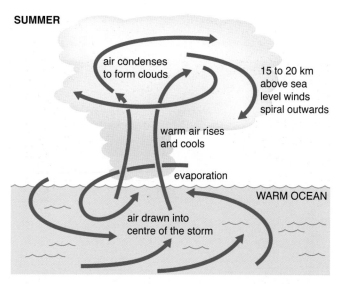

▲ Figure 10   The development of a hurricane

What are the hurricane hazards?

The main hazards associated with hurricanes when they make landfall are strong winds, often exceeding 100 mph (Hurricane Force is 75 mph), torrential rain and a rise in sea level called a **storm surge**. It is the storm surge, often up to 3 metres or more in height that causes the greatest amount of death and destruction to low-lying coastal areas. When Hurricane Katrina hit New Orleans, a storm surge combined with heavy rainfall to cause widespread flooding throughout the city (Figure 11).

▼ Figure 11   Flooding in New Orleans after Hurricane Katrina

How do people respond to hurricanes?

Immediately after a hurricane strikes there are a number of **short-term responses** by individuals and local communities. These include searching for family and friends, attending to injuries, finding food and water, and seeking shelter. These responses take place in the first few hours and days after disaster has struck, when conditions could be chaotic with no services working, such as electricity, water and sanitation.

In the days and weeks after a hurricane, **longer-term responses** kick in. These include restoring services, re-building homes and businesses, restoring law and order, re-opening schools and hospitals and generally trying to get the place back to normal. Most of the long-term responses are implemented by local or national government, or by global charity organisations.

Activities

5 Study Figure 9 on page 29. For this activity you will need a blank world outline.

a) Locate and shade the main hurricane formation areas shown on Figure 9.

b) Use the atlas map on pages 134–35 to label each of the hurricane formation areas. Label them on your map or add a key.
- West Pacific Ocean
- Arabian Sea
- East Pacific Ocean
- Bay of Bengal
- Southwest Pacific
- North Atlantic Ocean
- Southern Indian Ocean

c) Draw the common hurricane tracks using a colour of your choice.

d) What do all seven hurricane-forming areas have in common?

e) What do you notice about the location of hurricanes and the lines of latitude drawn on Figure 9?

f) Is the UK at threat from hurricanes?

g) Where do you think Hurricane Katrina was formed?

h) Why do you think hurricanes are rarely formed in the South Atlantic and the Southeast Pacific?

Case study: Cyclone Nargis, Burma (also known as Myanmar) 2008

On 3 May 2008 Cyclone Nargis struck the low-lying Irrawaddy delta region of southern Burma (Figure 12). It brought with it 80 mph winds and torrential rain, which caused considerable damage to homes and farmland. The most devastating aspect of the cyclone was a 3-metre storm surge that swept up the river channels of the delta inundating the heavily populated fertile farmland (Figure 13).

An estimated 100,000 people were killed and 1.5 million people affected by the disaster. Several entire villages were swept away. One small village alone – Pyin Su La – lost 40,000 people. Even the former capital Rangoon was severely affected, with electricity and water cut off.

Aid was slow to reach the people affected because the military government refused to allow aid agencies to operate in the immediate aftermath of the disaster. This undoubtedly led to a higher death toll than would otherwise have been the case.

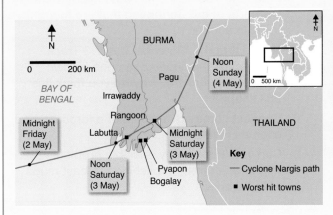

▲ **Figure 12 The path of Cyclone Nargis (May 2008)**

▲ **Figure 13 Destruction caused by Cyclone Nargis in Burma**

RESEARCH

Work in pairs, on a Powerpoint® presentation to describe why Cyclone Nargis affected so many people in Burma. Use the internet to find out more about what happened and why the hurricane had such a massive impact.

Here are some guidelines for your presentation:
- The focus of your presentation must be on *why* Burma was so severely affected, rather than simply what happened.

- You have a limit of ten slides only.
- One slide must show the track of the hurricane.
- Use powerful images to get your points across.

To get you started, access the Geographical Association's website at www.geography.org.uk/resources/cyclonenargis for an extensive selection of relevant links.

Can hurricane tracking reduce the hazard?

Look back to Figure 9 on page 29. Notice that hurricanes tend to follow certain common paths or tracks. This is because they are driven by the prevailing winds that blow in these tropical latitudes, together with the effects of the Earth's rotation which causes the slight curvature in the tracks.

The fact that hurricanes tend to follow similar tracks means that scientists can use computer models to predict the likely track of an individual storm. Satellite photographs (Figure 8, page 29) help to locate the precise position of a hurricane, providing scientists with important information to help them predict its future course.

Once predictions are made (Figure 14) it is then possible to issue warnings to enable people to be evacuated from coastal areas at risk. In the North Atlantic, there are two levels of warning. A **hurricane watch** is issued for areas possibly at risk. The higher level **hurricane warning** is issued for areas probably at risk. You can see these two warnings for Hurricane Gustav in Figure 14.

Whilst hurricane prediction is often quite accurate up to one or two days ahead, hurricanes can be erratic and sudden changes in course do happen. This can mean that places that thought they were safe, may suddenly and unexpectedly find themselves in the firing line!

Activity

6 Study Figure 14. It shows the position and predicted track of Hurricane Gustav on 25 August 2008.

a) In what direction is the hurricane predicted to travel?

b) How many miles is Hurricane Gustav expected to travel between 11am on Monday and 8am on Tuesday?

c) Convert this figure to a speed in miles per hour.

d) Which Caribbean country appears to be in immediate danger from the hurricane?

e) Describe the location of the areas that have received a 'Hurricane Warning'.

f) What do you think people living at the coast might be told to do as the hurricane approaches?

Further information on preparing for a hurricane can be found at www.fema.gov/hazard/hurricane/hu_before.shtm

g) Describe the predicted track of the hurricane from 8am Tuesday until 8am Friday. Identify the parts of the Caribbean that are thought to be in danger.

h) Notice that the 'Potential Day 1-3 Track Area' takes the shape of a cone (shown purple in Figure 14). Why do you think it is this shape?

i) Suggest some advantages of a forecast map such as Figure 14.

j) Can you think of any possible problems that might result from publishing forecast maps of hurricanes?

RESEARCH

Write a newspaper report describing the effects of Hurricane Gustav on the islands of the Caribbean. Use the official report from the National Hurricane Centre to get you started at www.srh.noaa.gov/lix/html/Gustav08/summary.htm. You will find plenty of other information on the internet including photos and maps.

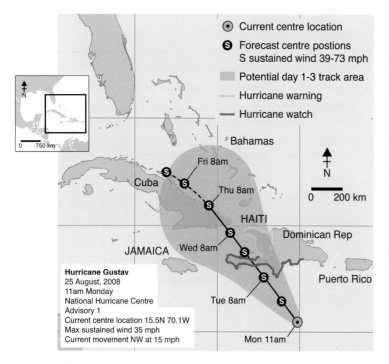

◀ **Figure 14   Predicted track of Hurricane Gustav, August 2008**

E Global warming

Look at Figure 15. It shows a polar bear stranded on an isolated block of ice in the Arctic. In recent years, there has been a dramatic decline in the extent of sea ice in the Arctic and this is now threatening the very survival of the polar bear. The melting of the Arctic sea ice is just one of many recent events that have highlighted the issue of global warming.

What is global warming?

Most scientists agree that the Earth is warming up. Look at the graph in Figure 16. Notice how the average global temperature has increased dramatically, particularly in the last 30 years. The 1990s were the warmest decade since the 1850s, with 1998 being the warmest year ever. Despite the dreadful summer in the UK, 2008 was the tenth warmest year on record! By the end of this century, average global temperatures are predicted to increase by between 1.4 °C to 4 °C. This may not sound very much, but it has the potential to significantly alter the world's weather, farming and ecosystems.

As the temperature of the oceans increases, **thermal expansion** (water actually expands when it is warm) of the water causes the sea level to rise. Thermal expansion, combined with the melting of ice on land, could cause sea levels to rise by 28 cm to 43 cm by the end of the century. This could lead to serious flooding in many low-lying coastal regions, such as Bangladesh. In the UK, sea level rise threatens many parts of the southeast, including London, where a new Thames Barrier will have to be constructed in just a few decades.

Many people believe that global warming is the most serious issue facing the human race. It will probably have a huge impact on your life!

▲ **Figure 15   A polar bear in the Arctic**

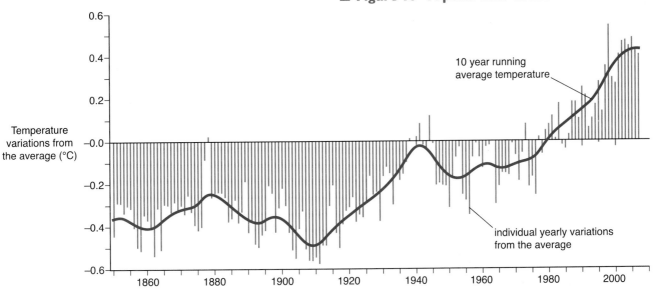

▲ **Figure 16   Global temperature graph showing variations from the long term average**

What is the evidence for global warming?

Apart from temperatures recorded over many years by thermometers, there are several other sources of evidence for global warming. One of the most interesting and revealing has involved the study of **ice cores** from Greenland and Antarctica (Figure 17).

When snow falls year on year, it builds up a record going back thousands of years. Water molecules and air trapped between the snowflakes can be analysed by scientists, to detect changes in temperatures and atmospheric gas concentrations at the time when the snow fell. By studying ice taken from different depths (the deeper the ice sample, the older the ice), scientists can build up a record of changes. The recent dramatic increase in global temperatures stands out very clearly when compared to trends going back thousands of years.

Other evidence includes the retreat of glaciers (Figure 18). Almost every glacier in the European Alps is retreating and this trend is mirrored elsewhere in the world. In the UK there is some evidence that the seasons are changing, with winters becoming less severe and spring starting earlier than in the past.

▲ **Figure 18   Glacier retreat**

Activities

7 Study Figure 16 on page 33.

 a)   1998 is the warmest year ever. How can this be seen on Figure 16?

 b)   What has happened to global temperatures after 1980?

 c)   What is odd about the temperatures in the early 1940s?

 d)   Describe the trend in the 10-year running average temperature since 1950.

 e)   Do you think this graph is convincing evidence of global warming? Explain your answer.

8 Study Figure 18. For this activity you will need a sheet of tracing paper.

 a)   Lay the sheet of tracing paper over the recent photograph of the glacier. Mark on the outlines of the mountains, the lake and the glacier. Add some labels to your sketch.

 b)   Now use a broken line to indicate the approximate position of the glacier in 1924.

 c)   Add a label to describe how the extent of the ice has changed between the two dates.

 d)   Do you think evidence of glaciers shrinking in size is good evidence of global warming? Explain your answer.

◀ **Figure 17   Scientist examining an ice core in the Antarctic**

What is causing global warming?

Most scientists believe that human activities are largely responsible for the recent warming trend. Look at Figure 19. It describes a vital atmospheric process called the **greenhouse effect** (so-named as it acts just like a greenhouse). The greenhouse effect involves gases (called greenhouse gases) in the atmosphere absorbing energy given off from the Earth. By retaining this heat, the lower atmosphere acts like a blanket keeping the Earth warm. Without the greenhouse effect it would be far too cold for us to survive!

In recent years, the levels of greenhouse gases (mainly carbon dioxide and methane) have increased. Many scientists believe that this is the result of human activities, such as the burning of fossil fuels in power stations, the dumping of waste in landfill sites, burning trees during deforestation and intensive agricultural practices (such as growing rice).

Many scientists believe that there is a clear link between the increased emissions of greenhouse gases and global warming.

▼ **Figure 19   The greenhouse effect**

Activity

9 Study Figure 19.

a) Make a large copy of Figure 19.

b) Write the following labels (where the blank boxes are) to identify the main sources of greenhouse gases:

   - nitrous oxides emitted from vehicle exhausts
   - carbon dioxide emitted from power stations
   - carbon dioxide emitted from industry
   - methane from farm animals
   - carbon dioxide released by deforestation and burning
   - methane gas released from landfill sites
   - methane given off by growing rice

c) Is the atmosphere heated up by incoming radiation (heat) from the sun or heat released from the Earth? Explain your answer.

d) Why does an increase in greenhouse gases lead to an increase in global warming?

e) Select *one* source of a greenhouse gas that you think could be easily controlled or reduced. Explain your selection and suggest what could be done.

f) Select *one* source that you think would be hard to reduce. Explain your choice.

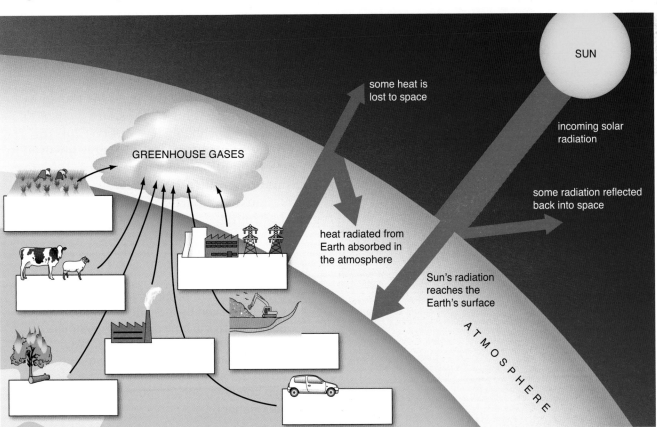

How can global warming be reduced?

There is no simple answer to the problem of global warming. However, scientists generally agree that we need to reduce the emission of harmful greenhouse gases, such as carbon dioxide and methane.

Global warming is an international problem that will require global solutions. An international agreement called the **Kyoto Protocol** aims to reduce emissions of carbon dioxide. Many countries across the world have signed the agreement setting targets to reduce their emissions. In order to meet their targets, countries are developing renewable sources of energy (Figure 20) and reducing harmful gas emissions from industries and vehicles. Unfortunately, the world's largest emitter of carbon dioxide, the USA, has refused to sign the agreement so far. In the next few years the Kyoto Protocol will probably be replaced by a new agreement.

▲ **Figure 21   A market in Taiwan**

At a local scale, individuals, households, schools and communities are striving to reduce greenhouse gas emissions. By conserving energy, we can reduce the need to burn fossil fuels. By re-using and recycling materials we can reduce what goes into landfill sites, where methane gas is produced as material rots. By using local building materials and eating local produce (Figure 21), we reduce the need for transport thereby reducing vehicle emissions.

Your school probably has an Eco-Club (or something similar) and it is probably involved in the government's Sustainable Schools Initiative. You should consider getting involved, so that you can play an active part in addressing the issue of global warming.

▲ **Figure 20   Renewable energy**

Activity

10 Work in pairs to produce a list of actions that could be taken by individuals and schools to help reduce the emission of greenhouse gases. Consider, for example, energy conservation, reducing waste and cutting down transport costs. Present your ideas in two columns, one for individuals and one for your school.

F Issue: What will be the effects of global warming?

The term 'global warming' tends to be linked to floods, famines, storms and the extinction of plant and animal species. But is a warmer world really going to be all bad news?

Greenland is witnessing some striking changes as temperatures rise. Local fishermen are able to access the sea earlier in the year and for longer, thereby increasing their catch (Figure 22).

Winters have become less extreme and the quality of life for some of the people seems likely to increase in the future. As the climate warms in the UK we will be able to grow cereal crops further north and, in the south, we will be able to grow Mediterranean crops such as grapes, olives and tomatoes. Tourism may increase and heating bills will go down in the winter. So, it is not all bad news.

▲ **Figure 22   Inuit people fishing in Greenland**

RESEARCH

The aim of this activity is to produce a PowerPoint® presentation, describing some of the possible effects of global warming on the UK and the rest of the world. Your target audience is pupils of your age.
- You should work in pairs to conduct your Internet research and design your presentation.
- You are only allowed a maximum of 12 slides for your presentation, so you will have to be selective.
- Try to include some written detail, as well as photographs and maps.

- Try to include some positive effects, as well as the more obvious (and more publicised) negative effects.

There is a huge amount of information on the internet and you will easily become swamped if you are not careful. Start by accessing the BBC Weather Centre at www.bbc.co.uk/climate/impact. This will give you a good overview of the possible impacts of global warming. Use a search to look for additional material and photographs in particular.

Global Tectonics

3

A Understanding the Earth: clues from below the sea

In Book 1, you learned how explorers such as James Cook travelled the world in search of new land. These explorers were able to record information about the new places they discovered, and cartographers (map makers) were able to create ever more accurate maps of the geography of the world. Mountains, rivers and volcanoes were plotted. However, nothing was known about what lay below the oceans! They were dark, cold and dangerous places beyond exploration.

Modern scientific research, together with the development of **submersibles** and satellite technology, has changed all this and we now know what lies below the sea. Take a look at Figure 1. It shows the Earth's surface without the oceans. Notice that there are some amazingly impressive features, such as mountain ranges as high as those on land, and tremendous gashes (or **ocean trenches**) up to 11,000 metres deep.

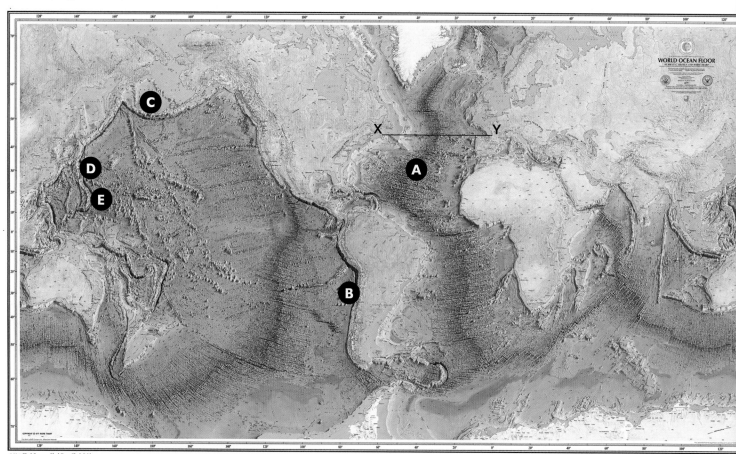

▲ **Figure 1   Map of the ocean floor**

Activities

1 Study Figure 1. Refer to the atlas map on pages 134–35.

   a) Describe the position and extent of the mid-Atlantic Ridge, A.

   b) Name an island that has formed along the mid-Atlantic Ridge.

   c) What are the names of the ocean trenches at B, C and D?

   d) Which of these ocean trenches is the deepest? State its depth.

   e) Find the height of Mount Everest in the Himalayas. Write down the height. Imagine that you could pick up Mount Everest and shove it into the Mariana Trench (E)! What depth of water would there be between the tip of the mountain and the bottom of the ocean trench?

2 In this activity you are going to draw a graph to plot the ocean floor beneath the Atlantic Ocean between Nova Scotia (X) on the east coast of Canada and France (Y) (see Figure 1). Look at the data in Figure 2. It lists depths of the ocean (distance from the ocean surface to the seabed) for a selection of points across the Atlantic Ocean.

   a) On a sheet of graph paper draw axes as shown on Figure 3. Make the horizontal axis as wide as you can and don't make the vertical axis too high.

   b) Use the data in Figure 2 to complete the graph by plotting the profile of the seabed. Mark each value with a cross and join up the crosses with a freehand line.

   c) Use a light blue colour to shade the Atlantic Ocean. Write the name of the ocean on your graph.

   d) Locate and label the Mid-Atlantic Ridge.

   e) Locate and label the following features:

   • **continental shelf**: a gentle slope at the edge of a continent

   • **continental slope**: a very steep slope between the continental shelf and the deep seabed

   f) Describe the shape, height and location of the Mid-Atlantic Ridge.

Longitude (° W)	Ocean depth (m)
64	0
60	91
55	132
50	73
48	3512
45	4024
40	3805
35	4171
33	3439
30	3073
28	1756
27	2195
25	3146
20	4244
15	4610
10	4976
05	4317
04	146
01	0

▲ **Figure 2 Ocean depth of Atlantic Ocean between Nova Scotia (Canada) and France**

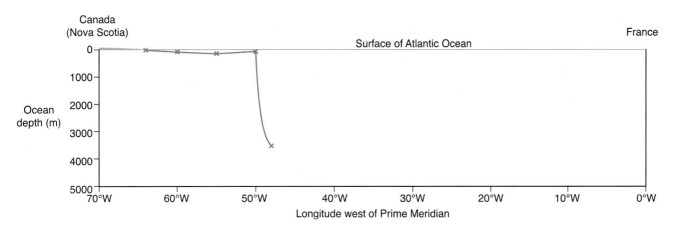

▲ **Figure 3 Cross-section across the Atlantic Ocean from Nova Scotia**

B The theory of plate tectonics

Ever since the first maps of the world were produced, people have tried to understand the formation of the Earth's major features and the causes of earthquakes and volcanoes. When studying maps, scientists observed that features such as mountains stretched over huge areas to form **mountain chains**, such as the Andes in South America (Figure 4). Similar patterns could be seen with earthquakes and volcanoes (Figure 5) and also with the major underwater features, such as ocean trenches (look back to Figure 1, page 38). Could there be a connection?

The connection is now explained by the recent theory of **plate tectonics**. This theory suggests that the Earth's outer layer (its crust) is divided into a number of very large 'slabs' called **plates**. You can see some of the Earth's major plates in Figure 6. Each plate is about 100 km thick, and it is able to move very slowly in relation to the plates alongside. The boundary line between two plates is called a **plate margin**. It is along these margins that the most earthquakes, volcanoes, mountains and ocean trenches are formed.

There are three types of plate margin:

● **constructive margin** – where two plates are moving apart

● **destructive margin** – where two plates are moving together

● **conservative margin** – where two plates are slipping alongside each other.

Activities

3 Study Figure 5. For this activity you will need a blank outline map of the world.

  a) Carefully locate the volcanoes shown on Figure 5 onto your world map. Use a symbol of your choice and explain it in a key.

  b) Use the atlas map on pages 134–35 to locate and name the following volcanoes onto your map:
   - Mt Fuji (Japan)
   - Mt Kilimanjaro (Tanzania)
   - Chimborazo (Ecuador)
   - Popocatepetl (Mexico)

  c) Now use Figure 6 to help you draw the major plates onto your map.

  d) Write the names of the plates and draw arrows to show their direction of movement.

  e) What do you notice about the location of volcanoes and the plates?

  f) Are there any exceptions to the general pattern?

  g) Mt Fuji volcano in Japan lies on the margin of which two plates?

  h) Are these plates moving towards each other or away from each other?

  i) What is rather odd about the location of Mt Kilimanjaro in relation to the plates?

4 Study the pattern of earthquakes in Figure 5.

  a) Do earthquakes and volcanoes tend to occur in the same places?

  b) There is a cluster of earthquakes along the west coast of South America. True or false?

  c) Most of these earthquakes occur in one mountain range. What is the name of this mountain range?

  d) Locate the Pacific Ocean. Notice that it is on both sides of the map! Describe the pattern of earthquakes in the Pacific region.

  e) Does the UK appear to be safe from major earthquakes?

  f) Look at Figure 6. Do all earthquakes occur at plate margins?

▲ **Figure 4   The Andes mountain range**

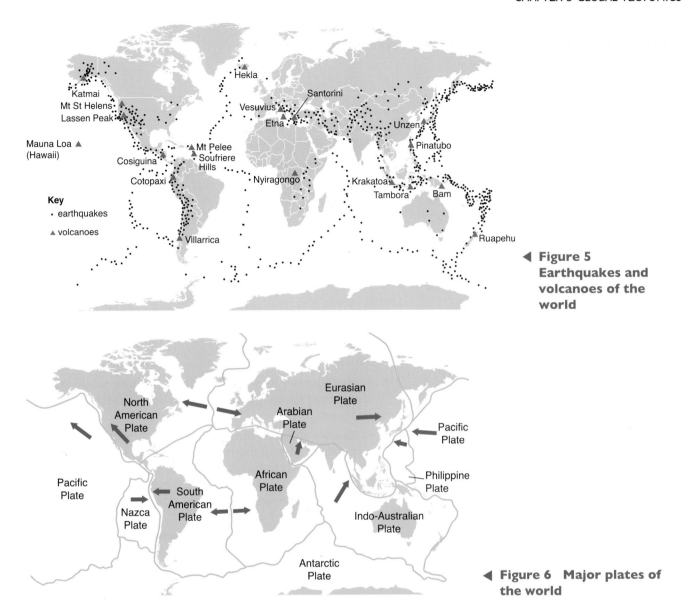

◀ **Figure 5
Earthquakes and
volcanoes of the
world**

◀ **Figure 6   Major plates of
the world**

 ICT ACTIVITY

Find out about the location of recent earthquakes. To do this access Active Earth at www.activeearth.org/googlemaps/EarthquakeMap.asp or the National Earthquake Information Centre at http://neic.usgs.gov/neis/qed. Consider these questions before attempting the activity that follows:

• Is there a pattern of recent earthquakes?
• Has there been a concentration of earthquakes in any particular area?
• Along which plate margins have most of the earthquakes occurred?
• Have there been any recent earthquakes in Europe? Where have they occurred?

Now complete the activity:
• Copy and paste the map onto your own Word® document.
• Draw and name the major plates using Figure 6.
• Add some labels to identify places that have experienced a lot of recent earthquakes.
• Add a title to your map.
• Now write a few summary sentences describing the pattern of recent earthquakes.

C Why do plates move around?

The world's plates move about very slowly (about the same speed as the growth of your fingernails) in relation to each other. At plate margins, pressure builds up to be released in sudden and unpredictable movements causing earthquakes. Plate movement also leads to the formation of volcanoes, mountain chains and ocean ridges. But why do the plates move?

Currents of heat originating from deep within the Earth called **convection currents** drive the movement of the plates. They work in much the same way as heat passing through a saucepan of cooled custard (Figure 7). When the custard cools, a thick skin forms on the surface. When the gas or electricity is turned on again, currents of heat (convection currents) begin to rise towards the surface through the custard. On reaching the surface, they cause the skin to split and move apart. Liquid custard now fills the gap, pushing the skin towards the edges of the saucepan.

The Earth's crust behaves in a similar way to the skin of the custard (Figure 8) in that currents of heat drive its movement. Of course, the movement of solid slabs of rock some 100 km thick is much more complicated than a saucepan of custard, but the principle is the same!

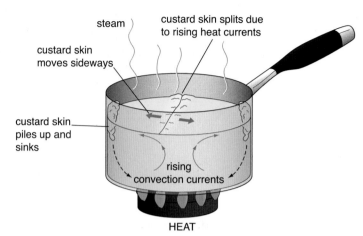

▲ **Figure 7 Convection currents in a saucepan**

Activity

5 Study Figures 7 and 8. This activity involves producing a storyboard for an animation made up of sketches based on Figure 7.

a) Draw a series of three simple sketches to show how currents of heat (convection currents) cause cooled custard skin to first split, and then move sideways. Figure 7 is the second of the three sketches, so you need to draw one before and one after. Add labels to show what is happening.

b) Now write a voiceover for the animation. This needs to make the connection between what is happening in the saucepan and how tectonic plates move. Remember that what happens in the saucepan is very simple and much faster than what happens in reality!

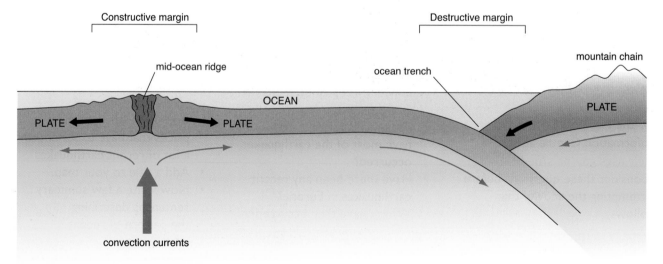

▲ **Figure 8 The causes of plate movement**

D Iceland: living on the Mid-Atlantic Ridge

Iceland lies on a constructive plate margin (see Figure 8). It is part of a submarine mountain chain called the Mid-Atlantic Ridge, which stretches for thousands of kilometres through the middle of the Atlantic Ocean (see Figure 1, page 38).

Did you know that Iceland is actually growing in size? As the two plates move apart the rocks crack, allowing molten rock called **lava** to flow out onto the surface (Figure 9). In this way, over millions of years, Iceland is slowly growing from the middle outwards.

Despite being at risk from the occasional earthquake and volcanic eruption, the people of Iceland gain a number of benefits from living on top of a plate margin. Just a few kilometres below the surface is a huge body of heat, that provides geothermal power, heats greenhouses and supplies most people in Iceland with cheap hot water and central heating (Figure 10).

Activity

6 Study Figure 11.

  a) Make a large copy of Figure 11 leaving plenty of room above the drawing for labels.

  b) Write the following labels in their correct places to indicate some of the benefits of living so close to a vast underground source of heat:
  - hard volcanic rocks used for building
  - swimming pools heated using natural heat from underground
  - electricity generated from steam
  - glasshouses heated to produce much of Iceland's fruit and vegetables
  - houses heated by hot water from underground
  - hot water circulated below pavements keep them de-frosted in the winter
  - natural geysers attract many tourists

▲ Figure 9 Lava eruption in Iceland

▲ Figure 10 The 'Blue Lagoon' heated by spent water from the geothermal power plant

▲ Figure 11 Benefits of Iceland's underground heat

E Living in the shadow of a volcano

Look back to Figure 5 on page 41 and find Mount Unzen in Japan. Notice that it is on a destructive margin where two plates are moving towards each other. The Philippine Plate is slowly sliding below the Eurasian Plate. As it does so, it melts to form molten rock called **magma**. In places, this molten rock escapes to the ground surface to form volcanoes (Figure 13). When magma reaches the ground surface it is called lava.

Mount Unzen is an active volcano on Kyushu, Japan's southernmost island (Figure 14). It last erupted in 1991. The eruption created a lava dome that then collapsed to form an avalanche of hot rocks and ash called a **pyroclastic flow**, which tore down the mountainside at speeds of up to 200 km/hour. Forty-three people were killed.

Over the next few years there were several smaller pyroclastic flows and, together with mudflows (called **lahars**), they destroyed over 2,000 homes and blanketed farmland and roads (Figure 12).

Look at the satellite photo in Figure 15. Locate Mount Unzen and the nearby city of Shimabara. Should the volcano erupt again (which is highly likely), some 51,000 people could be at risk.

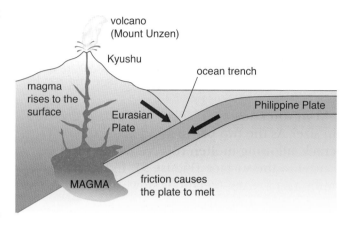

▲ **Figure 13   Destructive plate margin**

▲ Figure 14   **Location of Mount Unzen, Japan**

▼ **Figure 12   Pyroclastic flows and lahars caused by the eruption of Mount Unzen, 1991**

Mount Unzen

Activities

7 Study Figure 12. For this activity you will need a sheet of tracing paper.

   a) Lay your tracing paper on top of Figure 12 and secure it using paperclips.

   b) Use a sharp pencil to draw the mountainous skyline and the outlines of the main mountains. Mount Unzen has been labelled for you.

   c) Now show the flows of grey mud that have spread down the mountainside from Mount Unzen. These are the pyroclastic flows and lahars.

   d) Draw the outlines of some fields to the left of the photograph to indicate that this is an agricultural area.

   e) Locate a few houses to the right of the photograph to show that people live in this area.

   f) Now add a title to your sketch and additional labels to describe the effects of the 1991 eruption.

8 Study Figure 15.

   a) What is the evidence on the photograph that the pyroclastic flows and lahars flowed in an easterly direction from the volcano?

   b) Now look at Figure 12. In what direction do you think this photograph is looking?

   c) Do you think the shape of the coastline has been affected by eruptions from Mount Unzen? Explain your answer.

   d) Locate Shimabara. In what direction is Shimabara from Mount Unzen?

   e) Do you think Shimabara is at risk from a future eruption of Mount Unzen? Explain your answer.

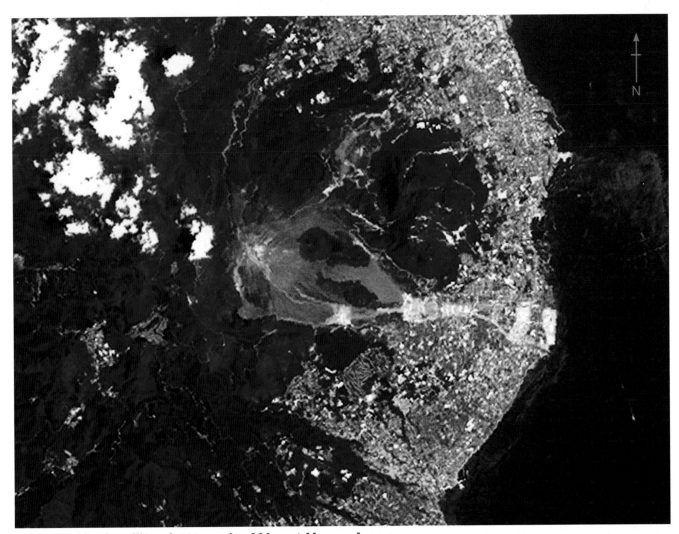

▲ **Figure 15   Satellite photograph of Mount Unzen, Japan**

Several measures have been introduced to reduce the risks associated with future eruptions of Mount Unzen.

- Hazard maps have been produced. These have identified those areas most at risk from pyroclastic flows and lahars.

- River channels have been dredged using remote-controlled machines. The enlarged channels will be more able to cope with a surge of ash and mud.

- Small dams called **sabo dams** ('sabo' means 'erosion control') have been constructed in river valleys to reduce the impact of a lahar by holding back sediment (Figures 16 and 17).

- Warning systems and evacuation procedures have been introduced for people at risk.

- Several instruments are in position to monitor the mountain. These include **seismometers** that measure earthquakes. Earthquakes can trigger landslides leading to pyroclastic flows.

Activities

9 Study Figure 17. It describes how sabo dams (Figure 16) can hold back sediment and reduce the impact of lahars. These two drawings are to be used as a short animation to show how sabo dams can reduce the impact of lahars. You have been asked to write a voiceover describing what is happening. You can use no more than 100 words. Share your voiceover with others in the class!

10 You work for the public information department at Shimabara's local government office. Some people in the town have become 'twitchy' about the dangers of a future eruption. They don't think that enough has been done to protect them. You have been asked to produce a single-page leaflet describing the various measures that have been adopted to reduce the hazard. Use the information in the text and the photos and diagrams to put together your leaflet. Use simple sketches and photographs from the internet to illustrate your leaflet.

▲ **Figure 16   Sabo dam in Japan**

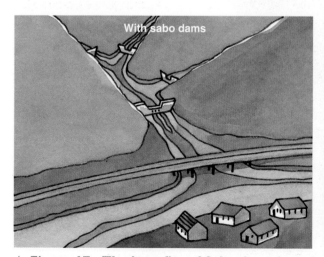
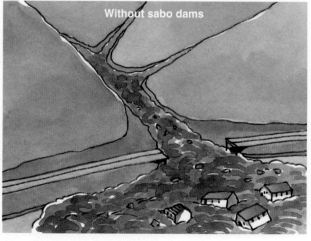

▲ **Figure 17   The benefits of Sabo dams in reducing the impacts of lahars**

F The 2010 earthquake disaster in Haiti

Shortly before 5pm local time on Tuesday 12 January 2010 a powerful earthquake struck Haiti in the Caribbean (Figure 18). Measuring 7.0 on the Richter scale, the earthquake's **epicentre** was just 25 km west of the country's capital Port-au-Prince, a city the size of Birmingham.

The violent ground shaking caused tremendous destruction (Figure 19). Some 230,000 people were killed and a million people made homeless, forced to live for several months in temporary camps on the outskirts of the city. People were pulled from the wreckage of their homes for several days after the event, many with terrible injuries. Some had to have limbs amputated in makeshift hospitals having been crushed in collapsed buildings.

In the immediate aftermath of the earthquake aid agencies and the US military provided much needed support for the victims of the earthquake in the form of clean water, food, shelter and medicines. Distribution was a major problem to begin with as roads were impassable and distribution points needed to be secure before food drops could be made. Large parts of Port-au-Prince and many of the surrounding towns and villages had to be completely re-built in the months after the earthquake.

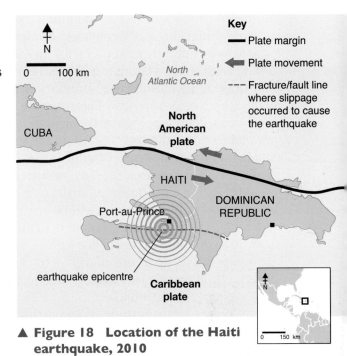

▲ Figure 18 Location of the Haiti earthquake, 2010

▲ Figure 19 The rescue effort after the earthquake

Activity

11 Study Figure 19.

   a) Describe what is happening in the photograph.

   b) Do you think the men are in any danger? Explain your answer.

   c) Describe the materials used to construct the buildings that have collapsed.

   d) Is there any other evidence of earthquake damage in the photograph?

   e) Notice that high wooden posts carry the power lines. How does this help to explain why electricity was cut off in most of the city after the earthquake?

   f) What do you think will be the immediate needs of the people in the photo during the next 24 hours?

   g) Do you think the buildings in the photo should be demolished and re-built? Explain your answer.

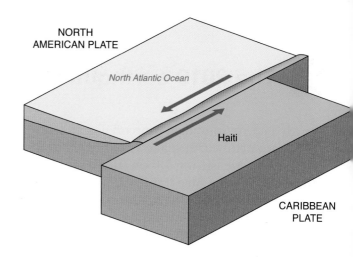

Earthquakes are terrifying events capable of causing tremendous destruction. Whilst Haiti had not suffered from a large earthquake for several hundred years, scientists had identified the area as being under threat. Despite this knowledge, the people were simply not prepared for an earthquake.

The reason why Haiti is at risk from earthquakes is because it lies close to the boundary of two plates, the North American Plate and the Caribbean Plate (see Figure 18, page 47). Running parallel to the main plate boundary are several major fracture zones called **faults**. It was along one of these that the sudden slippage occurred causing the devastating earthquake of 2010.

This type of plate margin, where one plate slides alongside the other, is called a **conservative** or **transform** plate margin (Figure 20). Pressure gradually builds up at this margin over many years to then be released as a sudden jolt. It is this that triggers an earthquake.

The power or magnitude of an earthquake is measured using the **Richter scale**. There is no upper limit to the Richter scale, although few earthquakes are greater than 9.0. The most powerful earthquake on record was a 9.5 earthquake that occurred in Chile in 1960. Earthquakes less than 3.0 are hardly felt.

▲ **Figure 20 A conservative transform plate margin**

RESEARCH

Find out more about the effects of the Haiti earthquake and the re-construction of Port-au-Prince afterwards.

1 **The effects of the earthquake.** Present your information in the form of a newspaper front page. You should include a dramatic and powerful image of the earthquake. Consider using eyewitness accounts. Describe what happened and the impacts on people and buildings. Include a map and diagram to show how the earthquake was caused. Think of a dramatic headline.

2 **The re-construction of Port-au-Prince.** Present this information in the form of a written report or Powerpoint® presentation. Describe how the city has been re-built after the earthquake. Consider housing, public buildings such as schools and hospitals as well as services such as electricity and roads. Has the city been improved by its re-construction? Is it less vulnerable to future earthquakes?

BBC website http://news.bbc.co.uk/1/hi/8455629.stm
Wikipedia http://en.wikipedia.org/wiki/2010_Haiti_earthquake

Activities

12 Study Figures 18 and 20.

a) Explain why the 2010 earthquake occurred in Haiti.

b) Earthquakes in Haiti are not very common. How might this fact have contributed to the scale of the disaster?

c) Most of the deaths resulted from the collapse of poorly constructed buildings. For example, some buildings were constructed using poor quality cement. They were not built to withstand ground shaking. Suggest reasons why many of the buildings were poorly constructed.

d) Most people in Haiti live on less than $2 a day. Suggest how the high levels of poverty might have contributed to the scale of the disaster.

13 Aid started to arrive soon after the earthquake struck. However, it took several days before it was distributed to the victims.

a) Why was it important to make aid distribution points in the city secure before supplies were brought in?

b) In the first few days, flights brought in search and rescue experts, aid and military personnel. With just one runway and little storage space, there was considerable congestion at Haiti's international airport and some flights had to be turned away. Which type of flight (search and rescue, aid or military personnel) do you think should have had priority immediately after the earthquake and why?

c) Work with a friend to construct a detailed list of the long term aid (months and years) that will be needed to help Haiti recover from the devastating earthquake.

G Tsunami 2004: the wave of destruction

On 26 December (Boxing Day) 2004, the seabed off the northwest coast of Sumatra, Indonesia (Figure 21) was shaken by one of the most powerful earthquakes ever recorded. Measuring 9.3 on the Richter scale, the massive earthquake shook the ocean with such ferocity that it sent waves in all directions towards the countries bordering the Indian Ocean. As these waves entered shallow coastal waters they grew in size to become monster walls of water called **tsunami** (Figure 22, page 50).

Activity

14 Study Figure 21. You will need to refer to the time zone map (Figure 10, page 7) to help you with some of these questions.

a) The earthquake occurred at 1am GMT (Greenwich Mean Time). What was the local time in northeast Indonesia when the earthquake occurred?

b) Which countries had been hit by the tsunami in the first two hours after the earthquake occurred?

c) What was the local time when the tsunami hit Sri Lanka?

d) Work out how fast the tsunami travelled on the way to Sri Lanka. To do this you need to use the scale to work out the distance from the earthquake to X. Now divide the distance by the time taken to give you a speed in km/hour.

e) Which part of Madagascar was hit first by the tsunami?

f) What was the local time when the tsunami first hit Madagascar?

g) Why do you think no one was killed or injured by the tsunami in Madagascar?

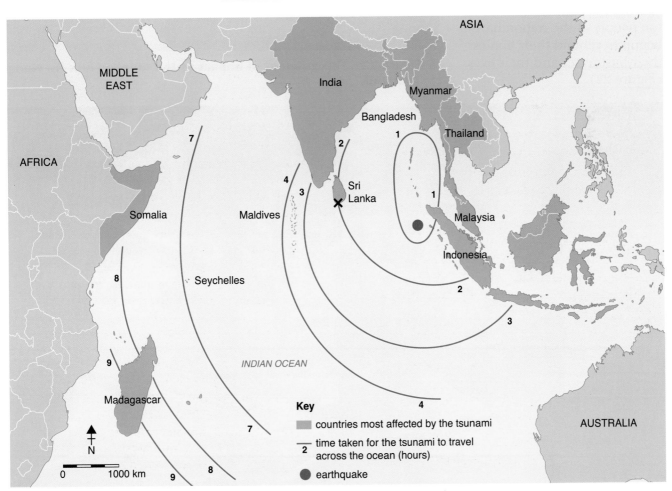

▲ **Figure 21** Countries affected by the 2004 Indian Ocean tsunami

Over a period of several hours, coastal regions of first Indonesia, then Thailand and India, Sri Lanka and East Africa, were overwhelmed by giant waves up to 20 metres high causing incredible destruction to towns, communications and natural environments (Figure 23). An estimated 230,000 people were killed and millions were left homeless. Agricultural land was inundated with salty water, shards of broken glass and the bodies of people and dead livestock. Water supplies were polluted, and services such as electricity were cut off for many weeks.

Aid poured into the region as people around the world watched the horrific images of the disaster captured by video and mobile phones. Very slowly the people of the region have begun to rebuild their homes, their businesses and their lives (Figure 24).

▲ **Figure 22   The moment of impact as the tsunami hits Ao Nang, Thailand**

▲ **Figure 23   Destruction caused by the 2004 tsunami**

Activities

15 Study Figure 22. Imagine that you were on holiday in Thailand when the tsunami struck and that you took this photo on your mobile phone. You survived the disaster and are showing the photograph to your friends on your return to the UK. Describe what it was like when the tsunami hit the coast. Describe what you saw and what you heard. How did you feel as the wave crashed onto the beach?

16 Study Figures 23 and 24.

a) Draw up a table with two columns headed 'short-term effects' and 'long-term effects'. Look carefully at Figures 23 and 24 and list the short-term and long-term effects of the tsunami on the people living in the area shown on the photographs.

b) Imagine that you are a member of a charity organisation. What would you do in the first few days after the tsunami to help people?

c) In the weeks after the disaster describe some of the things that you and your fellow charity workers would do to help the survivors. Give reasons for your suggestions.

d) Describe the features of the temporary kitchen constructed by the woman in Figure 24.

ICT ACTIVITY

1 Produce a PowerPoint® presentation to describe the impact of the 2004 tsunami on a country of your choice. You are limited to 10 slides only. Your presentation needs to include the following aspects:
- an opening slide to show the location of your chosen country
- photographs and text describing the effects of the tsunami on your country.

2 For your chosen country studied in question 1 above, use the internet to find out what has been done to reduce the impact of a future tsunami. Produce your findings in the form of a formal report using text, photographs and diagrams. There is a great deal of information on the internet about the tsunami so you need to search carefully and specifically (e.g. 'tsunami+sri lanka+aid'). Here are some websites to get you started.

BBC Special Report at http://news.bbc.co.uk/1/hi/in_depth/world/2004/asia_quake_disaster/default.stm

Guardian Special Report at www.guardian.co.uk/world/tsunami2004

▲ **Figure 24   Cooking in a temporary kitchen in Nusa, Indonesia**

H Issue: Rebuilding Nusa – how can communities recover from natural disasters?

Nusa is a small village in northern Indonesia. Read about what happened to Nusa when the tsunami struck in 2004 (Figure 25). In the early days after the disaster, the priorities were to bury the dead and tend the injured. Providing food, water and shelter were also important. Government help soon arrived, bringing food and medical supplies. Some foreign aid arrived too, but this was much less useful. In the weeks and months after the disaster, re-building began (Figure 24, page 51), and village life slowly got back to normal.

RESEARCH

The aim of this activity is to assess the usefulness of the help and support received in Nusa and suggest lessons that could be learned for the future.

   The information for this investigation can be found on the Guardian's website at www.guardian.co.uk/world/series/rebuildingnusa. Work through the following questions and then produce your final report.

1 Study the information in Figure 25. What were the immediate needs of the people in the hours following the disaster?

2 Read the website article 'Unwanted toys, lost crops' (20 January) and listen to the audio report (20 January). Make a list of the problems facing the village a month after the disaster. What help have the villagers received and how useful has it been?

3 Look at the photographs in 'In pictures: rebuilding Nusa (1)'. Select one or two photographs to illustrate your account so far.

4 Now read the article 'Village slowly gets back to normal' (23 February). What has happened in the village during the previous month? What are the challenges for the future?

5 Now write your report. Consider:
  • Was the aid supplied to Nusa in the first few weeks appropriate?
  • What lessons can be learned for future emergency aid?

Nusa is a medium-sized village about three miles from the sea, on the devastated west coast of the Aceh province of Indonesia.

● It has a population of around 1,300. Some 250 families live in the village.

● The tsunami killed 24 villagers. Twelve of the victims were children; six were aged 16–40 and the other six were over 40. Most people escaped by running into the hills.

● The village had 163 houses. The tsunami flattened 53 of them, and caused significant damage to 50 others.

● After the wave villagers found 150 bodies floating in their fields. They buried 42 of them in a mass grave. They left the others at the side of the road for collection.

● Some 70% of the villagers used to earn their living from farming. Rice, cassava, cloves and sweet potatoes are all grown here. The government employed 20%, while 10% worked in other professions.

● The village has a mosque, a primary school (which is no longer functioning because most of the teachers are dead), a cafe, a shop and a volleyball court (but the villagers haven't played volleyball since the tsunami).

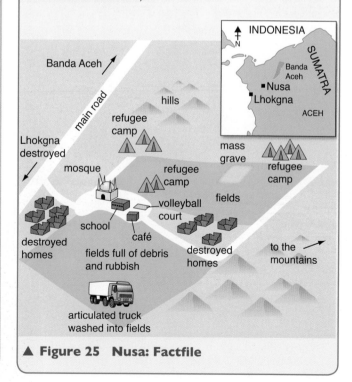

▲ Figure 25 Nusa: Factfile

Global Ecosystems

4

A Global biomes

Do you remember what the term ecosystem means? It is used to describe the interactions between living organisms and the environment where they live. In Book 1, we looked at some examples of local small-scale ecosystems, such as hedgerows and ponds. In Book 2, we studied ecosystems on a larger scale. These are called biomes. We looked at taiga forests and the Mediterranean biome, which cover large parts of Europe. In this book, we are going to consider some new biomes found elsewhere across the world, including tropical rainforests, deserts and coral reefs (Figure 1).

Look at Figure 2 on page 54. It shows the global distribution of the world's major biomes. Notice the trend of broad belts stretching west to east across the map. This reflects the broad pattern of climates (Figure 3, page 25). Information in the key above the map gives you a brief description of each biome and some of the issues affecting it.

Activity

1 Study Figure 2 (page 54). For this activity you will need a blank world outline and a large A3 sheet of plain paper. You are going to produce a colourful and informative poster describing the characteristics of the world's biomes.

   a) Make a careful copy of the world biomes in Figure 2 onto your blank map outline. Place this in the centre of the sheet of paper.

   b) Create information boxes around your map to give some details about each of the eight biomes shown on the map. Take time to plan your design. Your information boxes should include some details from Figure 2 together with a 'thumbnail' photo from the internet. You can of course search the internet for additional details too.

   c) Add a title to your poster and a key.

   Some good websites for information about global biomes include the following:

   www.blueplanetbiomes.org/world_biomes.htm
   www.ucmp.berkeley.edu/exhibits/biomes/index.php
   www.worldbiomes.com/default.htm

▲ Figure I Biomes found across the world

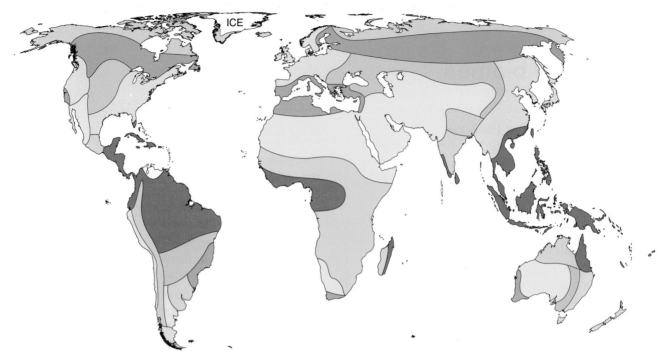

ICE

▲ Figure 2   Major global biomes

Key

Biome	Characteristics	Issues
Tundra	Low growing flowers and grasses which are able to survive the long, cold winters and short growing seasons	Damage caused by the exploitation of resources, such as oil in Alaska
Taiga Forest	Coniferous trees (including firs and pines) that are well adapted to cope with dry cold winters	Deforestation – wood used in industry and for making paper
Temperate deciduous forest	A mixture of trees (oak, beech and birch) and meadows which are well suited to a moderate climate with plenty of rain	Deforestation for agriculture, roads and urban developments
Mediterranean (Chaparrel)	Trees (such as olives and cork oaks) with thick bark and drought resistant qualities (deep roots, waxy leaves, etc) to cope with hot dry summers	Wildfires can cause damage in the summer; tourist developments can also be a threat to the natural environment
Grassland	Grasses well suited to the dry continental climate, usually used for grazing	Wildfires can be a problem in the summer; overgrazing can also be an issue in places, leading to soil erosion
Savanna	Scrubby vegetation adapted to dry hot conditions on the fringes of deserts	Overgrazing and deforestation for firewood can lead to soil erosion and the spread of the desert (desertification)
Rainforest	Lush dense forests that thrive in the hot and humid climate; huge range of plants and animal species	Deforestation for farming and industrial developments, such as mineral extraction
Desert	Few plants and low shrubs able to survive long periods of drought and intense temperatures	Overgrazing by goats, sheep and camels can lead to desertification

B Life in the Amazon jungle: tropical rainforests

If you could teleport yourself right into the heart of the Amazon rainforest in Brazil (Figure 3) you would be amazed. Within seconds you would be sweating due to the intense heat and the high humidity. You would probably need a torch to see where you were going, because the dense **canopy** of leaves and branches above your head would block out most of the sunlight. It would be very noisy, with the sounds of insects, birds and animals (such as howler monkeys). You will probably see huge vibrantly coloured butterflies, the size of your hand, flying past your nose. Underfoot, you would be walking on damp, decaying leaves. Watch out for the ants! There would be very few plants growing on the forest floor due to the lack of light. Oh, watch out for spiders and snakes too!

Tropical rainforests are found in a broad but broken belt across the world, from Central and South America in the west, through Africa, and into South East Asia and northern Australia in the east (Figure 2). They form the natural vegetation in the wet and hot climate that is found in these latitudes. Look at the bullet list to discover some interesting facts about tropical rainforests. You can see why so many people feel strongly that rainforests should not be cut down to make way for large-scale mining or farming.

Plants of the rainforest

One of the main characteristics of the rainforest ecosystem is the vertical layering of the trees and plants (Figure 4, page 56). It is rather like a multi-storey building, with several different floors! Each 'floor' has its own set of climatic characteristics and these determine the plants and animals that live there.

On the top 'floor' there are a small number of enormous trees such as the **kapok** (Figure 5, page 56). These trees push their way through the canopy layer in search of sunshine. They have large leaves to capture the sun's energy, and they are on stalks that can actually turn to follow the sun. The tips of the leaves are pointed (called 'drip tips') to allow the heavy rainfall to drip off them quickly. The plants at lower levels have adapted to survive in more shaded conditions.

- The trees of a tropical rainforest are so densely packed that rain falling on the canopy can take as long as 10 minutes to reach the ground.
- The forests of Central Africa are home to more than 8,000 different species of plants.
- More than 2,000 different species of butterflies are found in the rainforests of South America.
- About 2,000 rainforest trees are cut down every minute.
- 80% of the flowers in the Australian rainforests are not found anywhere else in the world.
- Rainforests contain two-thirds of the world's species of plants and animals.
- About 50 million tribal people live in the world's rainforests.
- In the moist rainforests of South America, sloths move so slowly that algae are able to grow in their fur.
- Rainforests supply many items that we use in our homes including rubber, cocoa, sugar and pineapples.
- 1 out of 4 ingredients in our medicine is from rainforest plants.
- An area the size of a football field is being destroyed each second.

▲ **Figure 3   The Amazon rainforest**

Activities

2 Study Figures 4 and 5.

a) The photograph in Figure 5 was taken from the ground. Use Figure 4 to help you estimate the height from the ground to the base of the canopy (the leaves and branches).

b) What is the name of the long thin plant that is growing up the bark of the kapok tree?

c) Why do you think it is climbing up the tree?

d) How does the texture (roughness) of the bark of the kapok tree help this plant to climb?

3 Study Figure 4.

a) Make a copy of the tall kapok tree in Figure 4.

b) Draw a vertical scale line to show how tall it grows.

c) Add the following labels to your diagram:
  • thick buttress roots to support the tree and help channel nutrient-rich water flowing down the stem to its roots
  • flowering plants (called **epiphytes**) growing directly on the tree bark
  • climbing lianas
  • thin bark because the wet climate does not require a thicker bark to retain moisture

d) Snakes move vertically between the layers to find food. Draw a snake on your sketch in a place where you would expect to find one.

e) Where on the kapok tree would you expect to find the greatest number of plants and animal species? Write your answer in the form of a label on your sketch. Give a reason for your choice of location.

4 Design a new type of emergent tree. Your tree needs to have the following adaptations:
  • strong roots to support the tree as it grows to over 40 metres in height
  • smooth bark to stop plants, epiphytes and lianas clinging to it
  • broad leaves to absorb maximum amounts of the sun's energy
  • a leaf stalk that enables it to pivot to follow the sun as it moves across the sky
  • a pointed leaf tip to let water drip off it quickly.

Draw a sketch of your new tree and a close-up sketch of its leaves. Add labels to identify its adaptations to the environment. Make up a name for your tree.

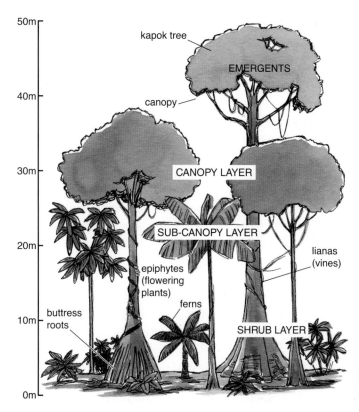

▲ **Figure 4   Typical structure of a tropical rainforest**

▲ **Figure 5   Looking up the trunk of a giant kapok tree**

People of the rainforest

People are an important part of the tropical rainforest ecosystem. People who belong to traditional tribes have to live in harmony with the natural environment in order to survive. Their lifestyle has to be sustainable.

The Yanomami is one of the largest tribes in the Amazon rainforest. They live in communities based around a central communal house called a yano. This is a large circular building made of vine and leaf thatch. In the centre of the building is a communal living area that can accommodate up to 400 people. Read about the way of life of the Yanomami in Figure 6.

Activity

5 Study Figure 6.

   a) **How do the Yanomami make use of the rainforest's plants?**

   b) **Do you think the Yanomami could be described as 'hunter gatherers'? Explain your answer.**

   c) **The women tend vegetable plots in much the same way that people in the UK have kitchen gardens or allotments. Why do they do this?**

   d) **Do you think the Yanomami have a varied diet? Explain your answer.**

   e) **Why is it important that the Yanomami live sustainably in their natural environment?**

   f) **Imagine that some of their traditional land were to be taken from them. What effects might this have on them?**

RESEARCH

The traditional way of life of the Yanomami is under threat. Mining and commercial ranching threaten to destroy the forest on which they depend. The charity Survival International supports traditional tribes worldwide.

Access their website at www.survival-international.org/home, click 'Tribes campaigns' then click 'Yanomami'.

Read through the various sections describing the threats to the Yanomami. There is a video clip to watch too. Make some rough notes using the following questions:

*   What are the development pressures on the rainforest?
*   Why is their way of life under threat? Consider how their culture might be under threat from intruders.
*   Do you think the traditional forestland of the Yanomami should be protected from development? Why?

Now present your information in the form of a report. This can be a handwritten report, or an electronic one (for example, a Powerpoint® presentation).

Complete this activity by writing a letter to your local MP, suggesting why the UK government should put pressure on the Brazilian government to stop harmful development in the rainforest and protect the Yanomami.

Additional information and photographs can be found at http://en.wikipedia.org/wiki/Yanomami
http://indian-cultures.com/Cultures/yanomamo.html
www.anth.ucsb.edu/projects/axfight/gallery.html

Each family has its own hearth where food is prepared and cooked during the day. At night, hammocks are slung near the fire which is stoked all night to keep people warm.

Like most Amazonian tribes, tasks are divided between the sexes. Men hunt for game like peccary, tapir, deer and monkey, and often use curare (a plant extract) to poison their prey.

Although hunting accounts for only 10 per cent of Yanomami food, amongst men it is considered the most prestigious of skills, and meat is greatly valued by everyone.

No hunter ever eats the meat that he has killed. Instead he shares it out among friends and family. In return, he will be given meat by another hunter.

Women tend the gardens where they grow around 60 crops, which account for about 80 per cent of their food. They also collect nuts, shellfish and insect larvae. Wild honey is highly prized and the Yanomami harvest 15 different kinds.

Both men and women fish, and timbó (or fish poison) is used in communal fishing trips. Groups of men, women and children pound up bundles of vines which are floated on the water. The liquid stuns the fish, which rise to the water's surface and are scooped up in baskets. They use nine species of vine just for fish poisoning.

The Yanomami have a huge botanical knowledge and use about 500 plants for food, medicine, house building and other artefacts. They provide for themselves partly by hunting, gathering and fishing, but crops are also grown in large gardens cleared from the forest. As Amazonian soil is not very fertile, a new garden is cleared every two or three years.

▲ **Figure 6 The Yanomami way of life**

Amazon mapwork

Figure 7 is a map extract of part of the Brazil/ Venezuela border in the Amazon rainforest. This is the main area where the Yanomami live.

Work through the following activities to discover more about the environment where the Yanomami live.

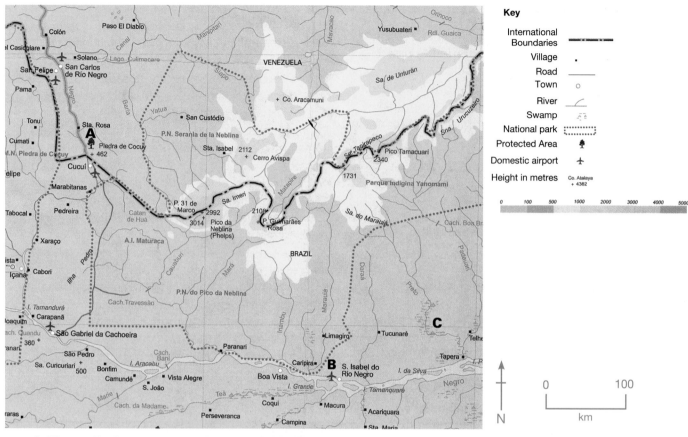

▲ **Figure 7   Amazon travel map 1: 3,300,000**

Activity

6 Study Figure 7.

a) The river at the bottom of the map is a major tributary of the River Amazon. What is its name?

b) What do you notice about the location of the majority of the settlements on the map? Why do you think they are concentrated in this area?

c) Notice that there is just one road on the map. Which two settlements does the road join? What is the distance between these two settlements along the road?

d) How do you think people reach these settlements from outside the area?

e) Apart from walking along the many forest tracks, how do you think the local people travel around the area?

f) Notice that the border of Brazil and Venezuela is hilly. What is the highest point above sea level in metres? Name the hill.

g) Most of the rivers on the Brazilian side of the border drain from north to south. True or false?

h) In what ways are the many rivers of use to the Yanomami?

i) What are the meanings of the symbols at A, B and C?

j) Is there any evidence that the Brazilian government has created a protected area for the Yanomami?

k) How does the map support the fact that the Yanomami live in a remote part of the Amazon?

C Living in extreme environments: hot deserts

Deserts are one of the most extreme environments in the world. The main characteristic of a desert is its **aridity** or lack of water. It is this lack of water that explains why deserts are usually sandy or rocky with only limited amounts of vegetation (Figure 8). Did you know that there are both hot deserts and cold deserts? Look at Figure 9 to see the location of the world's deserts.

Hot deserts experience extremely high temperatures in the summer, that often exceed 40 °C. Whilst winters are generally warm at around 20 °C, it can sometimes be cold enough for snow to fall. Temperatures plummet at night, as the clear skies allow rapid heat loss from the ground. Cold deserts have much colder winters, often with snow. Summers are not as warm as hot deserts.

Plants and animals of the desert

Despite the harsh environmental conditions, deserts are home to a great variety of plants and animals that have adapted to the lack of water and extreme temperatures. Look at Figure 10 on page 60. It shows who eats whom in the desert! It also describes some of the adaptations of the plants and animals that enable them to survive in the extreme conditions.

Activities

7 Study Figure 8. In this activity you will write a Haiku poem to describe the landscape shown in the photograph. A Haiku poem is a short poem made up of three lines. The first line has five syllables, the second line seven syllables and the third line five syllables.

  a) Look very closely at the detail in the photograph and make a list of words that describe the scene. Include words that describe your emotional responses to the photo and what you think it would be like to be there. Try to write ten words.

  b) Arrange your words to form a Haiku poem. The first line (of five syllables) could be 'Reddy, brown desert', for example. Write out your poem in full.

8 Study Figure 9.

  a) Make a copy of the deserts on a blank map of the world.

  b) Use the atlas map on pages 134–35 to identify and label the rest of the deserts on your map.

  c) Use the atlas map to draw the Equator and the Tropics of Cancer and Capricorn.

  d) Describe the location of the deserts. Do they occur at roughly the same latitudes?

  e) Most deserts are in the centre of the land a long way from the sea. How does this help to explain why they are very dry?

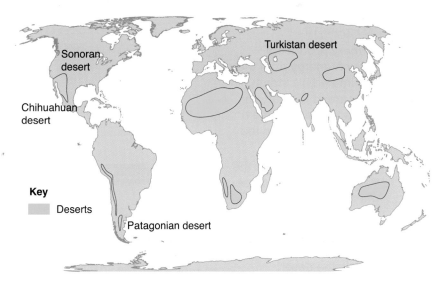

▲ Figure 9   Major deserts of the world

◄ Figure 8   Desert near Wadi Rum, Jordan

Desert kangaroo rat

This mouse-like rodent resembles a kangaroo, with its large hind legs. It is a nocturnal animal, living in cool burrows during the heat of the day and only venturing out in the cool of the night. Its large eyes help it to see during low light conditions. The burrows often have several entrances, and include food storage rooms and nests lined with plant leaves. The desert rat eats seeds, leaves, stems and insects, and it is able to extract water from the food it eats. When out of its burrow, it has to keep a watchful eye for predators (that include coyote, owls and snakes).

Coyote

A coyote is a large wild dog that is common in deserts. It feeds on a variety of foods, including fruits and berries, reptiles, rodents and insects. It has long ears, excellent eyesight and a very good sense of smell, and this helps it to find prey. The coyote's rusty brown colour disguises it in the desert.

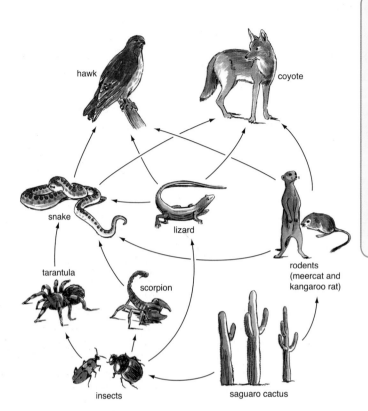

hawk   coyote   snake   lizard   rodents (meercat and kangaroo rat)   tarantula   scorpion   insects   saguaro cactus

◀ **Figure 10**
Desert food web

Activity

9 **Study Figure 10.**

 a) **Primary producers convert energy from the sun into edible starch. They are at the bottom of the food chain. Name a primary producer in the desert.**

 b) **Make a large copy of the Saguaro cactus and use the text to add labels to show how it is well adapted to the extreme environmental conditions.**

 c) **Why is the desert kangaroo rat nocturnal?**

 d) **Why is it important that the rat has a varied diet?**

 e) **How is the coyote well adapted to hunt?**

Saguaro cactus

This tall cactus is typically found in the deserts of western USA and Mexico. Some cacti are 200 years old! When it rains, its dense network of shallow roots quickly soak up the water. A long taproot searches for water deep underground. The ribbed skin of the cactus expands to hold water during wet periods. (Water is stored in the cacti's ribs.) Its thick waxy skin and spines (instead of leaves) reduce water loss. Nectar from the cactus feeds bees, ants and butterflies. Small rodents eat the cactus, and woodpeckers hollow out nests without causing any long-term damage to the plant.

 ICT ACTIVITY

Use the internet to discover some other adaptations of plants and animals that live in hot deserts. Choose one plant and one animal. Find a photograph or sketch, and add detailed labels (annotations) to describe the adaptations of your chosen plant and animal.
Here are some websites to help you get started, although a Google™ search 'desert plant adaptations' will reveal several sites for plants.
www.blueplanetbiomes.org/desert
www.kidcyber.com.au/topics/biomedes2.htm
www.animalcorner.co.uk/biomes/desert.html

People of the desert

The Bedouin are a desert tribe who live in parts of the Middle East. They are used to living in the extreme desert environment and have evolved a way of life that enables them to survive and prosper despite the hostile conditions.

The Bedouin are traditionally nomadic farmers. This means that they move across the desert with their herd of animals (usually camels, sheep and goats) in search of fresh pastures. Camels are their main form of transport (Figure 11) and they are extremely well suited to the desert conditions. The traditional shelter is the Bedouin tent (Figure 12). This is made from goat hair and is well insulated to keep the temperature cool during the day but warm during the winter nights. Goat hair expands when wet, so becoming waterproof when it rains. There is a large opening at the centre, which allows air to circulate as well as acting as a communal area for sitting and talking. The Bedouin are an extremely hospitable people who welcome friends and visitors with coffee and sweet mint tea.

Today, few Bedouin live in the traditional way, although they do retain many of their traditions. Most now live in brick or stone houses in small settlements, but they often have a traditional tent in the garden for use in the summer. Many still keep small numbers of animals.

▲ **Figure 11   Traditional Bedouin with camels**

▲ **Figure 12   Traditional Bedouin tent**

Activities

10 Study Figure 11.

   a) Can you think why camels are sometimes called 'ships of the desert'?

   b) Consider ways that camels are adapted to survive in the desert?

   c) Nowadays, 4x4 vehicles have replaced camels as the preferred means of transport. Can you suggest advantages and disadvantages of this trend? Consider the Bedouin people and the natural environment.

11 Study Figure 12.

   a) Draw a sketch of the traditional Bedouin tent.

   b) Add labels from the text to describe how it is well suited to the environment, and to the Bedouin way of life.

   c) Do you think a traditional Bedouin tent would be suitable for the UK climate? Explain your answer.

   d) The man to the left of the tent is wearing a traditional headscarf called a kaffiyeh. Suggest practical reasons why a headscarf is an appropriate item of clothing for living in the desert.

D Coral reefs: rainforests of the sea

Coral reefs are an example of an aquatic (water-based) ecosystem. They are found in warm shallow seas mostly in the tropics (Figure 13). Coral reefs are sometimes called 'rainforests of the sea' because they are home to a vast variety of species. For example, about 25 per cent of the world's fish live in coral reefs. They are incredibly beautiful environments (Figure 14), which explains why so many people choose to visit and explore them by snorkelling or diving.

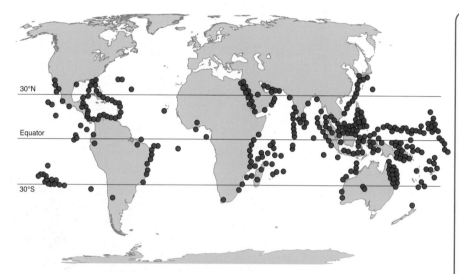

▲ **Figure 13   Global distribution of coral reefs**

- extremely rich ecosystems with over 4,000 species of fish and 800 species of coral
- provide protection to coasts from stormy seas (associated with hurricanes and tsunamis)
- provide food for local communities, such as fish, lobsters and shellfish
- coral is a source of lime used in building
- commercial fishing on coral reefs provides food and creates employment
- some reef organisms, such as coral and sponges, are used in medicine
- tourism provides jobs and is an important source of income to many countries

Activity

12 Study Figures 13 and 14, and the maps at the end of the book.

a) Describe the location of coral reefs.

b) Coral reefs are found in the following places, true or false?
- Red Sea
- Black Sea
- Caribbean
- Indonesia
- Madagascar
- Australia
- India
- Iceland
- South Island, New Zealand

c) Suggest one major reason to explain this pattern of coral reefs.

d) Look at Figure 14. Why do you think many people choose to visit coral reefs for their holidays?

e) Would you like to visit a coral reef? Explain your answer.

▲ **Figure 14   The diversity and beauty of coral reefs**

The coral reef ecosystem

The coral reef ecosystem is rich and complex (Figure 15). At the heart of the ecosystem are corals of which there are some 800 different species. Corals are tiny animals called **polyps** that live within an outer skeleton called an **exoskeleton**. As the exoskeletons grow and divide, a coral reef builds up on the seabed over a period of many hundreds of years.

Corals obtain most of their food from microscopic algae. These are the main primary producers in the ecosystem, as they are capable of converting the sun's energy into food. This explains why coral reefs are only found in shallow water, where light can penetrate to the seafloor. Apart from algae, coral reefs are rich in microscopic plants and animals called **plankton** as well as plants living on the seabed, such as seagrass. These are also primary producers. Fish, crustaceans, sponges and sea urchins feed on the primary producers. Carnivorous (meat-eating) fish, such as barracuda, feed on other fish. People make up the final part of the food chain by catching the fish! Scavengers which mostly live on the seabed eat plants and animals that die.

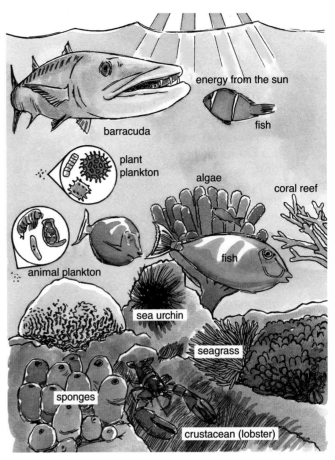

▲ **Figure 15   The coral reef ecosystem**

Coral reefs under threat

Coral reefs are very important ecosystems yet they are extremely fragile. Scientists are concerned about the health of the world's coral reefs. By 2011, an estimated 30 per cent of coral reefs will be damaged or destroyed. There are several reasons why coral reefs are in danger:

- Over-fishing using dragnets can kill coral, which is very sensitive to touch. If the coral dies, the ecosystem collapses.

- Pollution from sewage and waste from industry can kill coral.

- Hurricanes can cause physical damage to coral reefs.

- Silt washed down to the sea by rivers can reduce light, which is essential for the algae to thrive.

- An increase in sea temperature (due to global warming) can lead to 'bleaching', as corals expel algae which provide them with their food.

Activity

13 Study Figure 15.

a) Name two primary producers shown in Figure 15.

b) Name one animal in Figure 15 that grazes on seagrass.

c) Name one animal that grazes on plants that are growing on rocks on the seabed.

d) What is at the top of the food chain in Figure 15?

e) Why do you think coral reefs have so many fish living there?

f) If the water in Figure 15 were to become clouded with silt, what would be the likely effects on the ecosystem and why?

- Tourism can cause direct damage to corals, such as people treading on the coral or anchors scraping the reef as they attempt to moor the tourist boats.

- Coral reefs can be mined for sand or limestone.

Activity

14 Study Figure 16. It shows a stretch of beach on the Red Sea in Jordan, close to the port of Aqaba. Just offshore is a stretch of coral reef, which is beginning to become popular with tourists. At the moment tourism is very informal, but there is concern that mass tourism could lead to the ecosystem becoming harmed. You have been asked to produce an information board to be sited on the beach to inform tourists about the coral reef ecosystem. Your information board should contain the following:

- a sketch map showing the access point (Figure 18)
- brief information about the coral reef ecosystem and what to look for
- health and safety information (Figure 17), with simple sketches to help get your message across
- the importance of being responsible tourists and avoiding damage to the coral reef.

Design your information board using ICT.

▲ **Figure 16 Coral reef beach at Aqaba, Jordan**

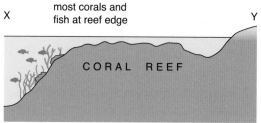

- Do not swim, snorkel or dive on your own.
- Do not walk on or touch the coral – it kills it!
- Do not take anything from the coral reef apart from photographs.
- Be careful in rough seas and be aware of strong currents.
- Do not swim outside the marker buoys.
- Coral is very sharp. If you get cut seek medical attention to avoid infection.

▲ **Figure 17 Health and safety on a coral reef**

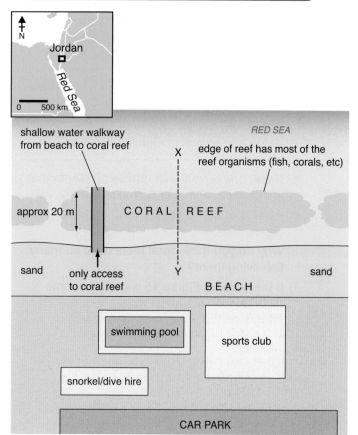

▲ **Figure 18 Coral reef resort at Aqaba, Jordan**

E Issue: How might global warming affect the Arctic ecosystem?

In recent years, there has been increasing concern about the effect that global warming might have on the fragile Arctic ecosystem (Figure 19), and on the lives of the Inuit people who live in the far north, on the coasts of Canada and Greenland.

The Arctic ice sheet is largely frozen seawater. In the summer, parts of the outer edges of the ice sheet break up and melt. In recent years, the extent of summer melting has increased alarmingly, and some scientists believe that

it won't be long before the ice sheet melts completely each summer.

Polar bears are the top predators in the Arctic ecosystem. They survive by hunting seals on the ice or on land (Figure 20). Whilst they are capable of swimming, they rarely catch seals in this way. As the sea ice gradually breaks up and disappears in the summer, the lives of the polar bears are threatened. How might this affect the Arctic ecosystem?

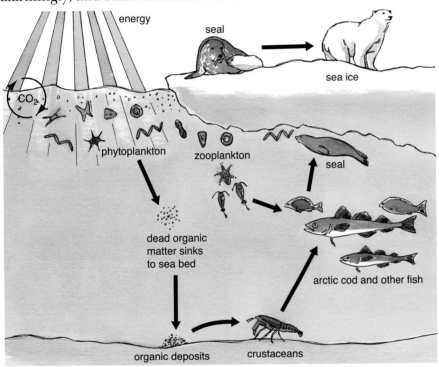

▲ **Figure 19 Arctic ecosystem**

▲ **Figure 20 Polar bear eating a seal**

RESEARCH

There are four aims of this activity:

1 to find out more about the Arctic ecosystem and, in particular, the role of the polar bear
2 to discover what effects global warming is having on the Arctic
3 to find out why polar bears are threatened with extinction
4 to suggest the possible effects on the Arctic ecosystem if the polar bear population is drastically reduced.

Work in pairs or small groups to carry out your

research. Then put it together in the form of a report. This could be in the form of a newspaper-style front page, a PowerPoint® presentation or TV news report. Here are a few sites to get you started.
Polar Bears International at
www.polarbearsinternational.org
BBC http://news.bbc.co.uk/1/hi/sci/tech/2642773.stm
Guardian www.guardian.co.uk/environment/2005/jan/31/climatechange.endangeredspecies
Map showing the range of polar bears in the Arctic
http://news.bbc.co.uk/1/hi/sci/tech/4447790.stm

People of the World

5

A The distribution of the world's people

Look at Figure 1. It is a map that shows the distribution or spread of the world's population. Notice in the scale that each square on the map represents a million people. You can see that the people of the world are not evenly spread. Some areas (such as north west Europe, Japan and parts of China and India) are much more populated than others (such as North Africa, Australia and Canada). Can you locate one other area with a high concentration of people and one with very few people?

Most people choose to live in areas that offer advantages. These include coastal regions where trade can take place between countries, fertile farmland on lowland plains (Figure 2) and areas where raw materials such as coal and iron can lead to the development of industry. The more hostile and remote parts of the world that experience a harsh climate or where the landscape is mountainous (Figure 3) are less hospitable places to live. These areas have fewer people.

▲ **Figure 2 Agricultural plain in Yunnan, China**

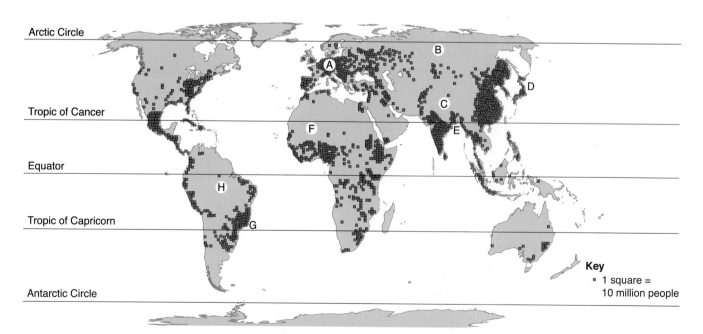

Key
■ 1 square =
10 million people

▲ **Figure 1 World population distribution**

Location letter	Statement number	Location area
A		
B		
C		
D		
E		
F		
G		
H		

▲ **Figure 5   Areas of high and low population**

▲ **Figure 3   The Andes**

Activity

1 Study Figures 1 and 4. Work in pairs for this activity.

a) Look at Figure 4. Sort the statements into two groups: one describing advantages of an area encouraging people to live there, and the other describing disadvantages.

b) Now make a copy of Figure 5. The location letters in the table are indicated on the map in Figure 1. Attempt to match the number of each statement in Figure 4 with the letter shown on Figure 1. Write your answer in the 'Statement number' column in your table. You may need to refer to the atlas maps in the back of the book to help you.

c) Now complete your table by identifying the geographical location of each of the areas A to H shown on the map. Use the atlas maps to help you with this. Be as detailed as you can, using country names, geographical regions and cities if appropriate.

1 Flat and fertile river valleys (e.g. Ganges) encourage farming and settlement

2 Hot desert environment with long periods of drought

5 Dense and remote tropical rainforest

7 Wealthy Far East industrial country with good transport networks and strong trade links with the rest of the world

3 Largely frozen ground with long dark winters

4 Large South American trading ports encourage industrial growth

6 Thriving European industrial region originally based on coal mining and other raw materials

8 Remote mountainous region with steep slopes and a very severe cold climate

▲ **Figure 4   Population distribution statements**

B Population density in Egypt

Population density is the number of people in a given area, usually a kilometre (sq km or km^2). Maps showing population density are commonly used to show the distribution of population, as it is easy to identify areas of dense and sparse population.

Egypt is a large country in North Africa bordering the Mediterranean Sea (Figure 7). It is well known for its archaeological treasures such as the Pyramids and the Sphinx. It was the home of one of the world's great early civilisations. Today it is a popular travel destination.

Egypt has a population of 81 million people, most of who live in a narrow strip alongside the River Nile and on the Nile delta (Figure 6). The River Nile is a vital lifeline for the people of Egypt in that it supplies drinking water and irrigation (artificial watering) for crops. It is also a major transport artery. In the past the river flooded regularly, depositing fertile silt on the floodplain. This accounts for the intensive farming here (Figure 8). On reaching the Mediterranean Sea, the River Nile forms a large **delta**. This large flat and fertile area of land encourages settlement. The busy ports of Alexandria and Port Said have led to the growth of trade and industry in this part of northern Egypt. Elsewhere much of the country is desert, with high summer temperatures and prolonged periods of drought.

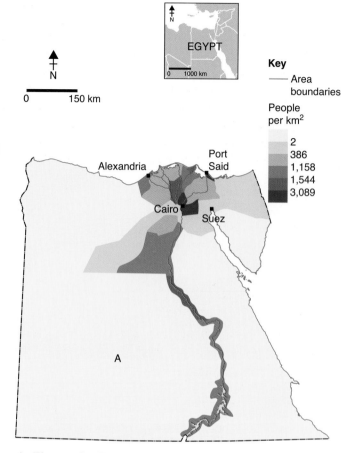

Key

— Area boundaries

People per km^2

2
386
1,158
1,544
3,089

▲ **Figure 6 Population density in Egypt**

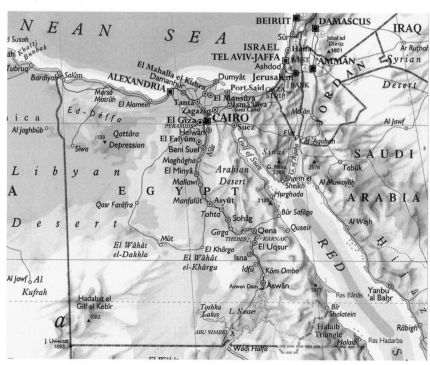

▲ **Figure 7 Egypt map extract**

Activities

2 Study Figures 6 and 7. Which of the following statements are true and which are false?

   a) Cairo has a higher population density than Alexandria

   b) The population density at Luxor (see Figure 8) is 386 – 1,158 per sq km

   c) Suez has a population density of less than 2 per sq km

   d) The River Nile has the same population density along its entire course as it flows through Egypt

   e) The Arabian Desert and the Libyan Desert have the same population density

3 Study Figures 6 to 8.

   a) Much of the valley of the River Nile is irrigated. What does this mean?

   b) What crops are grown in the River Nile valley and delta?

   c) How does the intensive use of land for farming explain the high population density along the River Nile?

   d) Can you suggest other reasons why the River Nile valley has a much higher population density than the land either side?

4 Study Figure 8. Notice that there are a number of oases in the desert.

   a) What is an oasis?

   b) Why do some trees such as date palms grow at oases?

   c) Is there any evidence on Figure 8 that oases are important for people and animals?

   d) Locate the administrative area A on Figure 6. Despite a number of communities living close to the oases (see Figure 8) the population density of this area is very low. Can you explain this?

ICT ACTIVITY

Locate the Siwa Oasis on Figure 8. A small town has grown up here.

- Use the internet to discover the characteristics of the oasis and find out why people have decided to settle here.
- Find a photograph to illustrate your account.
- Today it is a popular destination for adventure tourists. Why do people choose to visit the oasis?
- Would you like to visit the oasis? Give reasons for your answer.

A Google™ search will reveal several interesting sites. Here is one to get you started:

http://goafrica.about.com/od/egypttopattractions/ss/topsightsegypt_7.htm

Key

▨ irrigated farming	⬤ corn
▨ rough grazing/nomadic herding	▲ cotton
▢ desert	▢ rice
⬤ oasis	◯ sugar cane
■ citrus fruit	△ wheat

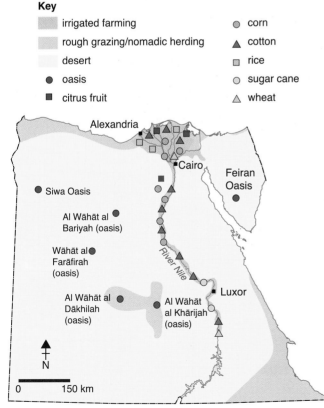

▲ Figure 8   Egypt land use map

RESEARCH

Carry out your own research study of population density for a country of your choice. Your study should include the following assets:

- a population density map of your chosen country
- a brief description of the map (where are the areas of high-density and low-density population?)
- a few sentences giving possible reasons for the patterns you have described (consider physical factors such as relief and climate as well as human factors such as land use and economic activity).

To start with, you need to conduct a brief internet search to consider the options. Some countries work better than others. You should select a country that has a varied pattern of population density, such as China, Australia, Peru or Brazil. Use a Google™ search, for example, 'population density map+peru'.

One very good site that contains maps for Arab countries is www.al-bab.com/arab/maps/maps.htm

C The world's growing population

In 2009, the world's population was estimated to be over 6.7 billion people. Did you know that every day the world's population increases by about 220,000 people? This is equivalent to a city the size of Southampton being created each and every day. In 2012, a population landmark will be reached when the 7th billion person is born.

As you saw in Figure 1 (page 66), the world's population is not spread evenly across the world. In fact, about 60 per cent of the world's population lives in Asia, with 37 per cent living in just two countries, China and India. All the countries of Europe (including the UK) only make up 11 per cent of the world's population.

Look at Figure 9. It shows the growth in the world's population during the last 2,000 years. Up until about 1800, the world's population grew only very slowly. This is because the number of births was being cancelled out by a high number of deaths, due to disease, wars and famines. Only since about the 1950s,

have global improvements in health care, water and sanitation led to a dramatic reduction in the number of deaths. With births remaining high in many parts of the world, the world's population has grown dramatically.

In the future, the growth of the world's population is expected to slow down. This is mainly because people will decide to have fewer children. One reason for this trend is that vaccinations and other medical improvements (Figure 10) mean that children are much more likely to survive than in the past.

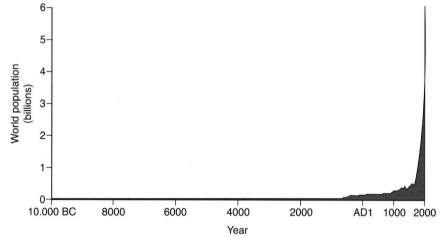

▲ **Figure 9 Population growth (10,000 BC to AD 2000)**

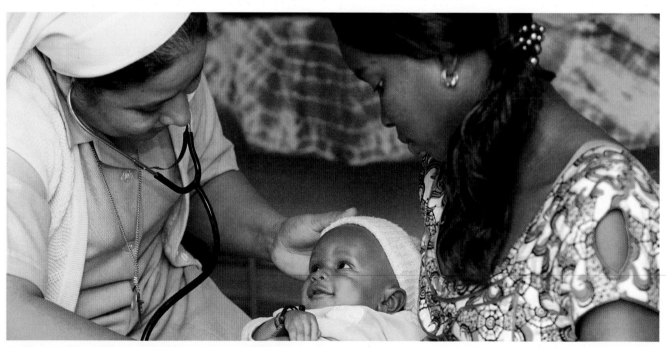

▲ **Figure 10 Village health centre in Africa**

Activity

5 Study Figure 11.

a) Draw your own graph to show the growth of the world's population since AD1 using the graph axes in Figure 12. Make sure that you keep an even time scale along the horizontal axis, e.g. 1 cm = 100 years.

b) Plot each population value in Figure 11 as a cross on your graph. Notice that the values in the table are in *millions* whereas the population axis on the graph is in *billions* (1000 million = 1 billion).

c) Join each cross with a freehand pencil line.

d) Complete the axes of your graph and write a title.

e) Use an arrow to locate the date when you were born. Do the same to show the birth date for one of your parents and grandparents.

f) Select the correct word from each pair to accurately complete the following sentences:

- From AD1 to 1500 the world's population grew very *slowly/rapidly.*
- The world's population started to rise very rapidly in *1850/1950.*
- In 1990 the world's population reached *5 billion/5 million.*

g) What date do you think the world's population will reach 10 billion?

h) What are the challenges facing the world as the population continues to grow?

Date	World population (millions)
1	170
1000	310
1500	425
1800	980
1850	1260
1900	1650
1950	2400
2000	6070
2050	8900 (estimate)

▲ Figure 11   World population growth

ICT ACTIVITY

Access the world population clock at http://math.berkeley.edu/~galen/popclk.html. This shows a current estimate of the world's population and the 'live' clock allows you to see how it is expanding.

- Watch the clock for a few seconds and then try to estimate the increase during a single minute. Use the 'freeze' function to stop the clock and then re-start it after a minute has passed. How accurate were you? Compare your result with that of others in your class.
- Now estimate the population total at the end of a 30-minute period. Once again compare your result with others in the class.
- How many hours/days would it take for the number of new people added to the world's population to equal those living in your home town or city?

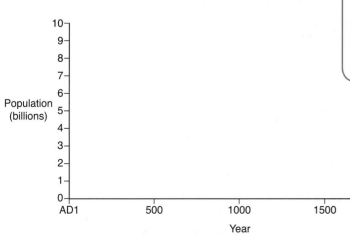

▲ Figure 12   World population growth graph axes

D Bangladesh: a country with a rapidly growing population

In 2008, the population of Bangladesh was estimated to be about 153 million. Not only is it one of the most populous countries in the world, but it is also one of the most rapidly growing. Look at Figure 13, which shows the growth of population in Bangladesh. Notice that the population grew slowly up until about 1960. Since then it has grown very rapidly.

The current population growth rate in Bangladesh is just over 2 per cent a year, which is equivalent to an extra 3 million mouths to feed. It is one of the highest growth rates in the world, and presents huge challenges in one of the world's poorest countries.

Why is the population growth so high?

Population change depends on two main factors: **birth rate** and **death rate**. The birth rate is the number of live births per 1000 population. The death rate is the number of deaths per 1000 population. The figures are always expressed 'per 1000 population', so that comparisons can be made between countries with different size populations.

If the birth rate exceeds the death rate, there will be a **natural increase** in the population. If death rate exceeds birth rate, then there will be a **natural decrease** in the population. The only other factor affecting the total population of a country is migration in or out of the country.

Look at Figure 14. Notice that in 1910, the birth rate was 54 per 1000 and the death rate was 46 per 1000. Birth rate minus death rate, leaves 8 per 1000, and this is the natural increase. Look down through the table and notice that death rate drops dramatically whilst the birth rate stays high. This high natural increase explains the rapid growth of Bangladesh's population.

Death rates in Bangladesh have fallen due to improvements in health care, particularly of the very young and the elderly. Food supply has increased and more people enjoy the benefits of piped water and sanitation.

The birth rate figures in Bangladesh have remained high for several reasons:

- early marriages – many women marry in their late teens and have large families

- tradition – there is a strong tradition for women to have many children

- contraception – this has not been freely available or widely accepted by people

- high infant mortality – a high death rate of babies has meant that women have chosen to have several children in the hope that a few will survive

- low status of women – in the past women were expected to stay at home and look after children rather than following their own careers.

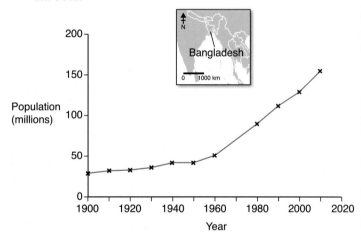

▲ Figure 13   Population growth in Bangladesh

▶ Figure 14   Bangladesh – birth rates and death rates

Date	Birth rate (per 1000)	Death rate (per 1000)	Natural increase (per 1000)
1910	54	46	8
1920	53	47	6
1930	50	42	
1940	53	39	
1950	49	41	
1960	51	30	
1970	48	19	
1986	39	12	
2008	29	8	

What problems are created by a high growth rate?

The rapid increase in population has put pressure on the resources in Bangladesh. Many people flock to the towns and cities in search of employment, better quality housing or services (such as schools and hospitals). As Bangladesh is a poor country, it is unable to cope with the growth in demand for these basic needs and, as a result, many people end up living in squalid conditions in squatter settlements (see page 79).

What can be done to reduce the rate of population growth?

Since the mid-1950s, **family planning** has been adopted as the main way of trying to slow Bangladesh's population increase. The Family Planning Association of Bangladesh was founded in 1953. It aims to encourage women to have smaller families, by promoting later marriages and the use of contraception. It sees family planning as a basic human right. A lot of its work is done through educating both men and women in schools.

▲ **Figure 15   Girls at school in Bangladesh**

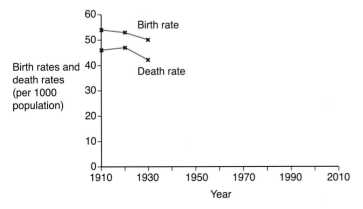

▲ **Figure 16   Graph for Activity 7**

Activities

6 Study Figure 14.
   a) Complete the final column by calculating the natural increase values. The first two have been done for you.
   b) What is the evidence that Bangladesh's population starts to grow rapidly from the 1960s?
   c) Is there any sign that the population growth rate is slowing down?
   d) Why is natural increase not always an absolute measure of population change in a country?

7 Study Figure 16. It is a graph plotting information for birth rate and death rate in Bangladesh using the data in Figure 14.
   a) Make a large copy of the graph axes in Figure 16.
   b) Use the data in Figure 14 to complete two lines, one showing the birth rate and one showing the death rate. Use two different colours to make the lines stand out clearly.
   c) Use a colour to shade the natural increase.
   d) Can you think of any possible reasons why the death rate increased in 1920 and 1950?
   e) Use your graph to predict the birth rate in 2020.
   f) Assume that the death rate remains at 8 per 1000 in 2020, what will be the natural increase in 2020?

8 For this activity you will need to work in small mixed groups (boys and girls), if possible. Imagine that you are a small team working for a family planning organisation in Bangladesh. Your team has been asked to go into a local village school in a remote part of the country where birth rates are still high. You will have an hour to talk to a group of about twenty 13- to 14-year-olds about the importance of education and the value of later marriages and smaller families.
   a) Look back at page 72 to remind yourself why some women in Bangladesh have large families.
   b) Discuss what important information you wish to get across to the young people.
   c) Consider how you are going to deliver your message (there is no electricity in the school, although paper and pencils are available). You could consider group work, role-play, drama, poems, poster making, etc. Try to be creative, but practical. The most important thing is to get your message across in a way that young people will understand and accept.

E Refugees: the world's forgotten people?

Try to imagine that you and your family are at home one evening. There is an unexpected loud and frantic knocking on your door. There is a lot of shouting. Your parents go to the door to find a distraught neighbour insisting that you all leave immediately because people are being kidnapped, raped and killed.

You grab a few items that are close at hand, and leave your home with the lights on and the doors open. Later that evening you learn that your house has been burned down. Your family, along with thousands of other people, walk night and day in search of somewhere safe to stay. You have very little food and water. It rains. It is cold. Eventually you end up in a foreign country where the local people do not want you and do not speak your language. This is what it is like to be a refugee.

Refugees are people who have been forced to move away from their home country to save their lives or avoid being persecuted. Wars, ethnic conflicts and natural disasters, such as floods or volcanic eruptions, can force people to leave their homes in search of safety in another country.

In 2002, Nyiragongo volcano in the Democratic Republic of Congo erupted (Figure 17). Hundreds of thousands of people were forced to move from the nearby city of Goma as streets were engulfed by lava flows and houses burned down. Most of the refugees crossed the nearby border into Rwanda (Figure 18). Here they settled into temporary refugee camps (Figure 19) where they had to cope with appalling conditions, with little water, food or medical support. Cholera was a constant threat as water sources became polluted. When the eruption ceased, most returned to Goma to try to rebuild their shattered lives.

There are about 10 million refugees in the world today. The United Nations High Commission for Refugees (UNHCR) supports refugees throughout the world and many charity organisations (such as Oxfam and the Red Cross) offer help and support. Most often it is the poor and innocent who become refugees. All they want is to be able to return home.

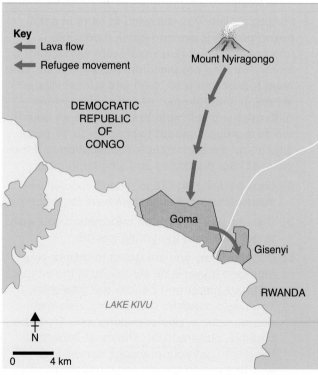

▲ **Figure 17   Location of Nyiragongo volcano in DR Congo**

▲ **Figure 18   Congolese refugees leaving Goma for Rwanda**

Activities

9 Study Figures 18 and 19.

   a) Look closely at Figure 18 and describe the possessions that the refugees have decided to take with them.

   b) Make an estimate of how many refugees are shown in the photograph.

   c) Imagine that you were part of the group of refugees in the photograph.
- How do you feel about leaving your home?
- What will you miss most?
- What possessions have you brought with you and why?
- How do you feel as you settle down in a camp in a foreign country?
- Is there anything that you are looking forward to?

   d) Describe the likely conditions in the refugee camp shown in Figure 19.

   e) How could conditions be improved?

10 Study Figure 20. For this activity you will draw a number of vertical bars to represent the information in Figure 20 on a world map. You will need a blank world outline.

   a) Work out an appropriate scale (e.g. 1cm = 200,000 people). The horizontal width of your bars should be constant.

   b) Use a pencil and ruler to carefully draw the bars, locating the base of them as close to each country as possible.

   c) Use a colour of your choice to shade each bar. Use a single colour for all the bars.

   d) Write the names of each country onto your map and add a title at the top.

   e) See if you can discover why so many people have been forced to leave Afghanistan.

▶ **Figure 19 Refugee camp in Rwanda after the eruption of Nyiragongo volcano in 2002**

RESEARCH

1 Carry out a research project into a recent refugee migration of your choice. You may like to consider refugees from Darfur in Sudan, Iraq or Afghanistan. You may be interested to find out more about the people fleeing from Burma following the tropical cyclone in 2008.

Before you decide, have a look at the following websites to give you some ideas:

- United Nations High Commission for Refugees at www.unhcr.org/home.html
- Wikipedia's entry on refugees at http://en.wikipedia.org/wiki/Refugee

2 Use a software package (such as Movie Maker®) to create a 'photo diary' describing life in a refugee camp. There are a huge number of photos available on the internet and you will have no difficulty finding some. Your task, however, is to select just six that you think show the life in a refugee camp most effectively. For each of your chosen photographs, you need to write a short caption describing the scene.

Take a look at the excellent BBC refugee photo diary of life in a refugee camp in Tanzania at http://news.bbc.co.uk/hi/english/static/in_depth/world/2001/road_to_refuge/foreign_land/photo1.stm

Country	Refugees
Afghanistan	2,108,000
Iraq	1,451,000
Sudan	686,000
Somalia	464,000
DR Congo	402,000
Burundi	397,000
Vietnam	374,000
Turkey	227,000
Angola	207,000
Burma	203,000

▲ **Figure 20   Top ten countries of origin for refugees (2007)**

F Issue: Should China's one-child policy be relaxed?

One of the most controversial policies for slowing down population growth is China's **'one-child' policy**. It was introduced in 1979, in response to a rapidly growing population and fears that the country might not be able to feed itself in the future.

Under the policy, couples have been encouraged to marry later and restrict the size of their families to one child only. Those couples that have conformed to the policy have been given free education and other benefits. Those who have not conformed have lost these benefits, and some have been forced to have abortions or be sterilised. Neighbours and government officials have kept a watchful eye on couples to make sure that they have conformed to the policy.

In some respects, the policy has been very successful. It has prevented 400 million births, and China has been able to develop rapidly and feed itself without the burden of these extra mouths to feed. However, with boys favoured over girls, many girls have been abandoned to end up in orphanages (Figure 21) and some have even been killed. The younger Chinese population has become distorted with far more boys than girls. Think about the implications of this, when people wish to get married. As an only child, some boys have become spoilt too.

The government is beginning to consider relaxing the policy. It has already done so in some rural areas and following the 2008 Sichuan earthquake, where large numbers of children were killed.

▲ **Figure 21   Baby girls in an orphanage in China**

RESEARCH

The aim of this activity is for you to decide whether the one-child policy should be relaxed. To do this you need to carry out the following steps:

- Consider the advantages of the policy for the future. Will China continue to benefit from the one-child policy in the future?
- Find out more about some of the problems associated with the policy. How will the current population structure affect Chinese life in the future? Consider employment, marriage and relationships, retirement, etc.
- How could the policy be relaxed? Should the sanctions be less serious or different rules apply to different parts of China? What would happen if the policy were abandoned completely?

Work in pairs to consider these questions and try to reach an agreed conclusion. Present your views as part of a class debate. Imagine you need to convince a panel of experts. At the end of your class discussion, you could take a vote or agree on a joint class policy for China.

Here are some websites to get you started:

http://news.bbc.co.uk/1/hi/world/asia-pacific/7000931.stm

www.timesonline.co.uk/tol/news/world/asia/article3452460.ece

www.bbc.co.uk/schools/gcsebitesize/geography/population/manpopchangerev2.shtml

Additional links can be found at http://delicious.com/geographyalltheway/china_one_child

Global Cities

6

A   Global cities

Did you know that in 2008, for the first time ever, more than half of the world's population lived in towns and cities? By 2030, this is expected to rise to 60 per cent (it is predicted to amount to 6 billion people). So, why do so many people choose to live in urban areas?

Many people migrate to urban areas (towns and cities) because they face problems and difficulties in rural areas (the countryside). People are 'pushed' away from rural areas by lack of services, unemployment, food shortages and a lack of opportunities. In contrast, people are 'pulled' to urban areas by better job opportunities, services and entertainment.

The increase in the proportion of people living in towns and cities is called **urbanisation**. This growth is partly due to migration from rural areas, but it is also due to the growth of the population within an urban area. Many of the people moving to a city are young adults. As they have their families, so the city population expands.

Rank	City	Population (millions)*
1	Tokyo, Japan	34.4
2	Jakarta, Indonesia	21.8
3	New York, USA	20.1
4	Seoul, South Korea	20.0
5	Manila, Philippines	19.6
6	Mumbai (Bombay), India	19.5
7	Sao Paulo, Brazil	19.1
8	Mexico City, Mexico	18.3
9	Delhi, India	18.0
10	Osaka, Japan	17.3
11	Cairo, Egypt	16.8
12	Kolkata (Calcutta), India	15.0
13	Los Angeles, USA	14.7
14	Shanghai, China	14.5
15	Moscow, Russia	13.3
16	Beijing, China	12.8
17	Buenos Aires, Argentina	12.4
18	Guangzhou, China	11.8
19	Shenzhen, China	11.7
20	Istanbul, Turkey	11.2

(* rounded to one decimal point)

▲ **Figure I   The top 20 largest cities in the world (2006)**

Activity

1 Study Figure 1. It shows the top 20 cities in the world by population size. Calculating the size of a city is extremely difficult and if you do a Google search you will find quite a lot of variation. In this activity you are going to draw a map, locating each city in its correct place using a proportional bar to represent its population. You will need a blank world map outline.

a) Decide on a vertical scale to use in drawing your bars. This will depend on the size of your map, but 1 cm = 10 million will work reasonably well. Keep the horizontal width constant for all bars.

b) Use an atlas (or the map on pages 136–37) to locate each city in turn on your map. Mark its position with a pencil cross. Use a pencil to draw a bar, with its base as close to the city's location as possible. Use your vertical scale to draw the bar to the correct height.

c) When you have completed all the bars in pencil, colour them in using a single colour of your choice. (Use one colour only because all the bars are showing population.)

d) Complete your map by writing a title and explain the scale of the bars in a key. You could include some thumbnail photos from the internet to illustrate your map.

e) Are the cities spread evenly across the world or clustered in certain areas?

f) Are there any cities in the top 20 that you have never heard of before? Write them down.

g) Are there any cities that you would have expected to be in the top 20?

Look at the images in Figure 2. They show some of the characteristics of living in towns and cities. We will explore some of the problems and opportunities illustrated by the photos later in this chapter.

Activity

2 Work with a friend for this activity. Study the images in Figure 2.

a) Draw up a table with two columns, one with the heading 'Advantages of living in cities' and the other 'Disadvantages of living in cities'. List the advantages and disadvantages shown in the images in Figure 2.

b) Using a different colour, try to add some additional advantages and disadvantages to your table, using your own experience and general knowledge.

c) Discuss (and try to agree on) the top five most important advantages and disadvantages.

d) Compare your results with others in your class.

e) Can you guess where the places are in the photos?

▲ Figure 2   Cities around the world

B   Living in the slums: Mumbai, India

Mumbai is India's largest city, with a population estimated to be about 20 million people. It is one of the world's 25 '**megacities**', having a population of over 10 million people, and it is growing at a rate of about 500,000 every year! Situated on the west coast of India, it is an important port and industrial city. Many of India's top financial companies have their headquarters in Mumbai. It is also home to the country's film and television industry, known as 'Bollywood'.

In common with cities all over the world, Mumbai is a city of contrasts. There are wealthy districts with skyscrapers, shopping malls and modern apartment blocks (Figure 3). There are also extensive areas of poor quality slum housing, where many people live in appalling conditions. In this section, we are going to concentrate on life in the slums.

▲ Figure 3   Modern Mumbai

What is a slum?

Slums are run-down areas of a city often characterised by poor quality housing and a lack of services, such as fresh water, sanitation and electricity. Low-income groups, or those who are disadvantaged, usually occupy these areas. In some parts of Mumbai, slums are older properties that have fallen into disrepair and have been sub-divided to house large numbers of people.

Elsewhere in the city, shacks made using wood and other scrap materials, often with corrugated iron roofs, form extensive areas of housing (Figure 4). These unplanned and informal areas of housing are sometimes called **bustees** (the Indian term for shanty town).

In Mumbai, an estimated 55 per cent of the population live in slums, covering just 6 per cent of the area of the city. You can see why people in these areas have to live in such crowded and cramped conditions.

Activity

3 Study Figure 5.

a) Make a list of the types of material that have been used to build these homes.

b) Why do you think there are so many buckets and storage containers?

c) Is there any evidence that the people living here have access to electricity?

d) What other services do you think they have to cope without?

e) Mumbai is often affected by heavy rain (the monsoon). How might the monsoon cause problems for people living in these homes?

f) Considering the problems, why do you think people have chosen to live here?

g) What do you suggest could be done by the city authorities to improve the living conditions of the people living here?

▲ **Figure 4　The Dharavi slum in Mumbai**

▲ **Figure 5　Low income (slum) housing in Mumbai**

C Dubai: city in the desert

Dubai has become one of the most popular destinations for long haul travel in recent years. You may well have heard about its huge shopping malls and the ambitious new coastal developments, such as the Palm Deira and The World (Figure 6). For all its recent glitz and glamour, Dubai has a long history as an industrial and trading centre, which makes it a very interesting place to study.

Dubai is one of seven 'emirates' that make up the United Arab Emirates (Figure 7). Each emirate has some independence in passing its own laws and maintaining its facilities in much the same way that Scotland, Wales and Northern Ireland have some powers within the United Kingdom.

Dubai is the most populous of the emirates, with a population of about 2.3 million people. This is midway between the population of Manchester and Birmingham. Dubai is a linear city that stretches for several kilometres along the coast of the Arabian Gulf (Figure 8).

Look closely at Figure 8 and notice that the city has a number of **functional areas** where certain types of land use dominate. There is an industrial area to the south of the city, a financial (money) district in the centre and a maritime (sea) district in the north. Can you spot any others?

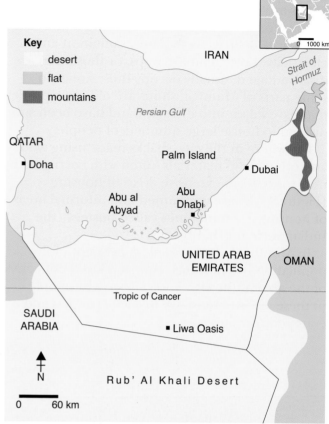

▲ **Figure 7 Map of United Arab Emirates**

▼ **Figure 6 Palm and World coastal developments in Dubai**

Activities

4 Study Figure 8.

a) Using the scale, work out the length of the built up area on the map from Ajman in the north to Mina Jabal Ali in the south.

b) Most people who visit Dubai from abroad arrive by aeroplane. How many international airports are there on the map extract?

c) What evidence is there on the map that Dubai is a 'desert city'?

d) What is the name of the industrial area in the south of the city?

e) Locate Dubai International Financial City. Describe its location in Dubai.

f) If you were interested in sport, what activities could you take part in or watch in Dubai?

g) If you were interested in nature and wildlife, what attractions are there in Dubai?

h) What new developments are planned in the area and where are they to be located?

i) Try to explain the choice of location of these new developments.

5 Study Figure 6 and Figure 8. Locate the offshore developments on the map, including the Palm Deira and The World.

a) Why do you think they have been constructed?

b) Do you think they are a good idea? Explain your answer.

c) Suggest another themed coastal development for the Arabian Gulf and give reasons for your choice. Include a simple sketch to show your design.

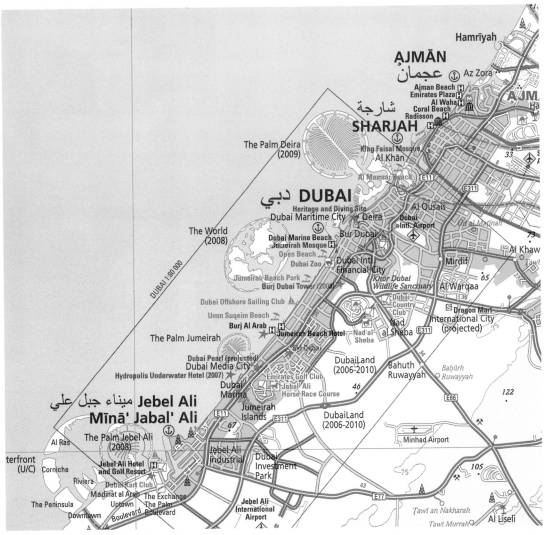

▲ **Figure 8 Dubai map extract**

The many faces of Dubai

Dubai grew up as a trading centre in the 19th century, establishing strong links with India. It became famous as a centre for pearls, which were exported around the world. From 1892, Dubai was a British Protectorate, which meant that the British were very much involved in the security and development of the emirate.

In 1966, oil was discovered in Dubai. Workers poured into the city from India and Pakistan to work in the oil industry and the city started to grow rapidly, both in size and regional importance. Foreign industrial and financial companies were encouraged to move to Dubai and the city started to become very wealthy.

In recent years, the potential for tourism has been exploited, given the excellent climate and the attractions of the coastal and desert environments. Today, Dubai has many faces: historical, industrial, financial and tourism. The busy and colourful city centre (Figure 9) reflects the range of different functions in Dubai.

Activity

6 Study Figure 9.

a) Which people in the photo are tourists? How can you tell?

b) What is being sold on the stalls?

c) What evidence is there that this is a modern shopping mall?

d) Would you like to visit this shopping mall? Explain your answer.

▲ **Figure 9 Open air shopping mall in Dubai**

Activity

7 Study Figure 10.

a) Why do you think the city of Dubai grew up on the banks of Dubai Creek?

b) Use the scale to calculate the width of Dubai Creek at its widest point.

c) How can people travel from one side of the Dubai Creek to the other?

d) Locate the Deira Fish, Meat and Vegetable Market on the coast. Do you think this is a good location for the market? Explain your answer.

e) Now locate the Hyatt Regency hotel just along the coast. In what direction is the hotel from the market?

f) Why do you think this location was chosen for the Hyatt Regency hotel?

g) There are a large number of mosques in Dubai. What does this suggest about the religion of the people in Dubai?

h) Notice that there are many car parks in the city centre, suggesting that lots of people use cars. Use the map to suggest why driving in Dubai is not very easy.

i) Locate the Bastakia area on the south bank. This is an historical area built by Persian traders in the 19th century. It is now a conservation area with narrow alleys and restored buildings. Why is it important to conserve areas of historical interest in cities?

j) You and your family are staying at the Hyatt Regency hotel (lucky you!). Your family has hired a taxi to take you to Bastakia. Assume that you will be travelling on main roads. Describe the likely route that you will take from your hotel to Bastakia. Use road names and directions in your answer.

k) Use the Internet to help you discover the meaning of the words 'souq' and 'dhow', which are used on the map. Both are important features of life in Dubai.

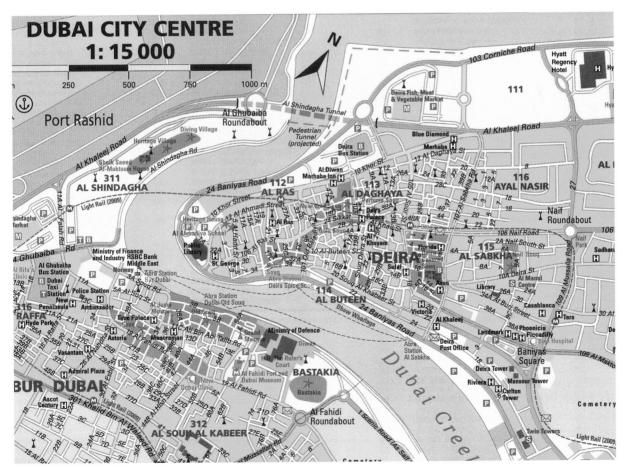

▲ **Figure 10   Dubai city centre map**

Challenges facing the 'desert city'

Dubai is located in a hostile desert environment. It experiences a hot and largely dry climate, where temperatures regularly exceed 40 °C, especially in the summer months. Rainfall is restricted to the winter months of December, January and February. This can take the form of very heavy storms.

People living in Dubai have developed ways to cope with this extreme climate. In the past, the narrow alleyways provided welcome shade and relief from the heat of the sun. Buildings were designed with **wind towers** (Figure 11) to trap and re-direct breezes to help keep the houses cool. Nowadays, most cars, homes, hotels and shopping malls have air-conditioning but this uses up a great deal of energy.

With a low annual rainfall and a huge demand for water, particularly for industry and tourism, water management is a major issue in Dubai. In the past, water came from underground aquifers, but these sources are unsustainable given the current low rainfall totals.

Today, 97 per cent of Dubai's water comes from the sea! It is processed at desalination plants located along the coast, where the salt is extracted to create drinkable freshwater. It is an expensive way of supplying water, and the government are encouraging people to conserve and reuse water. There are ambitious plans to build three giant reservoirs to store rainwater, to help support the rapidly growing demands in the city.

In January 2010, Dubai suffered from **flash flooding** following torrential storms (Figure 12). Although such events are rare, planning to cope with severe rainfall events is important as the city continues to expand.

Activities

8 Study Figure 11.

   a) Make a simple sketch of the wind tower in Figure 11.

   b) Use arrows and add labels to describe how the wind tower traps and diverts breezes downwards into the building to help circulate air and keep it cool.

   c) Notice that the street is in shadow. Why does this happen? Use a simple diagram to support your answer.

   d) Do you think the buildings were deliberately designed to create shaded streets? Why?

   e) The wind towers have been restored and are now part of a conservation area in Dubai. Why do you think this area is popular with tourists?

9 Study Figure 12.

   a) Imagine you are in the car in Figure 12. You are a local radio reporter. Write a short script for an audio clip that you will be making for a broadcast describing the impacts of the flood.

   b) Suggest other likely effects of the flash flood in Dubai. Use Figure 10 on page 83 to help.

   c) Water is a very precious resource in Dubai. Can you suggest what could be done to store water from storm events such as this?

   d) Do you think Dubai should spend money on flood defences? Explain your answer.

▲ **Figure 11   A wind tower**

▲ **Figure 12   Flash floods in Dubai, March 2010**

D Sustainable towns and cities

If you have seen the 'Dark Knight' or any of the 'Batman' movies, you will be familiar with the fictional city of Gotham (Figure 13). With its tall dark overcrowded buildings, narrow crime-ridden streets and smoky polluted air, Gotham is the nightmare city of the future. Whilst Gotham is fictitious, it is not so far removed from parts of the world's largest cities, where the litter-strewn streets become 'no-go' areas after dark, and where breathing the air is equivalent to smoking a packet of cigarettes a day. Such cities are unsustainable, because they are damaging the environment and creating a range of social and economic problems, such as crime, drugs and social unrest.

Increasingly, planners wish to create sustainable cities that enable people to live and work together in pleasant surroundings, and without damaging the environment. Sustainable cities promote public transport (e.g. buses, trams, metros), walking and cycling. They have extensive green areas, both public parks and private gardens where food crops can be grown and animals reared.

Sustainable cities are light, bright and vibrant places with local markets and a strong sense of community. Waste and pollution is minimised and self-sufficiency encouraged. Water is reused and energy conserved.

▲ **Figure 13 Gotham City**

Examples of sustainability in towns and cities

Bangkok, Thailand

There are many parks and tree-lined streets in Thailand's capital, Bangkok. Look at Figure 14 and notice that several raised beds have been constructed on a rooftop to grow vegetables.

▶ **Figure 14   Rooftop gardening in Bangkok, Thailand**

London, UK

Like Bangkok, London is also quite a green city with many parks and open spaces. Where space is in short supply people have started to create roof gardens (Figure 15).

▲ **Figure 15 Urban sustainability in Islington, London**

Activities

10 Study Figure 13 on page 85.

   a) Describe some of the characteristics of Gotham City.

   b) Why is it a good setting for the 'Dark Knight' and the 'Batman' films?

   c) In what ways is Gotham City an unsustainable city?

11 Study Figure 14 on page 85.

   a) What evidence is there in the photo that Bangkok is a 'green city'?

   b) What do you think the man in the photo is doing?

   c) Consider how cities like Bangkok could address transport and energy issues in order to become more 'green'.

12 Study Figure 15.

   a) What do you think the man is doing? (Hint: think honey!)

   b) How does he reach the roof?

   c) Describe the other uses of the roof in the photo.

   d) Do you think it is a good idea to use roofs for gardens? Explain your answers.

RESEARCH

Curitiba is described as Brazil's 'ecological city'. In 2007, it was identified as one of the top three 'Green Cities' in the world. Located in southern Brazil, Curitiba has a population of about 1.8 million. Urban planning over the last few decades has resulted in the city being a model of sustainability. Write a short project on Curitiba as a sustainable city. Consider the following aspects:

- urban transport
- parks and gardens
- recycling and waste management
- quality of life and social inclusion (where people are encouraged to live and work in mixed communities).

Include a map to show the location of Curitiba in Brazil and use photographs to illustrate your project. You will find several links at www.geographypages.co.uk/curitiba.htm

E Issue: How can the design for Dongtan 'ecotown' be improved?

In 2005, plans were released for the construction of the world's first brand new 'ecotown'. Located on an island, 45 km north of Shanghai, Dongtan was due to become the world's first truly sustainable town (Figure 16). It was to be one of a number of sustainable cities to be built by the Chinese. But, by 2009, little progress had been made due to high costs and local opposition. Even if Dongtan fails to be built, the idea is an interesting one and worthy of consideration.

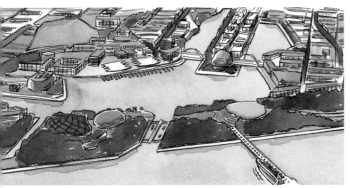

▲ **Figure 16 Artist's impression of Dongtan ecotown**

Activity

13 You should work in pairs for this activity. The aim of the activity is for you to design an improved version of the original plan for Dongtan (Figure 17). You need to make your city as sustainable (green) as possible using ideas from this chapter. You need to keep costs as low as possible too.

- You must not build on the protected natural wetland, but can open up the area for visitors.
- You must consider energy supply, water, waste and recycling, local food production, employment, housing and transport.

Remember: your aim is to improve on the design in Figure 17, although you can retain any features that you consider to be good.

Complete your design on a large sheet of plain paper using colours to make it look attractive. Display your design as a class and vote on the best one!

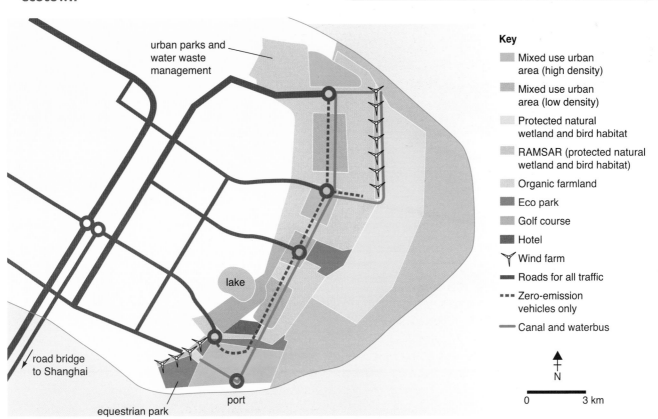

▲ **Figure 17 Dongtan 'ecotown', China**

Global Food and Farming

7

A Farming around the world

In Books 1 and 2, we studied examples of farming in the UK and Europe. We will now study the amazing range of farming elsewhere in the world.

Farmland is used to grow crops for food, such as rice in the Philippines, wheat in the USA (Figure 1), bananas in the Caribbean (see page 94) and tea in Sri Lanka. It is used to grow crops for industry, for example Australian grapes are grown to make wine and Malaysian palm oil is used to make edible and industrial oils. Flowers are grown in Kenya (see page 98) to be exported for wedding bouquets in Europe. Animals such as beef cattle (Figure 2), sheep and chickens are reared on grass pastures or, occasionally, more intensively in huge sheds. Some crops are even grown as a renewable energy resource, such as sugar cane to fuel Brazil's cars.

There are several important issues involving farming around the world. Some of these we will consider in this chapter and others you may like to research yourself:

- Should there be worldwide standards of animal welfare banning intensive animal rearing?

- Should farming be organic?

- Should farm workers be paid a better wage?

- Should farmers be paid a fairer price for the crops they grow?

- Should productive land be used to grow industrial cash crops (rather than food) when people in the world are starving?

- Should chemicals be used on the land?

▲ **Figure I   Cereals in the USA**

▲ **Figure 2   Beef ranching, for example in Argentina**

Activities

1 Work with a friend for this activity. Study the photos in Figures 1 and 2. Look closely at *each* photo and attempt to answer the following questions.

   a) What is being grown or produced?

   b) What are the people doing in the photo?

   c) Are many people involved or is it mainly mechanised?

   d) What is the landscape like?

   e) Are there any clues in the photo to suggest the climatic characteristics?

2 Play the game 'Alphabet Run' for world farming. Try to suggest a farm product (output) for each letter of the alphabet. For example, A could be alpaca or alfalfa. Run this activity as a classroom competition: score 1 point for each correct answer and 3 points for a correct answer that no other group in the class has thought of.

ICT ACTIVITY

Having played the 'Alphabet Run', you should now be aware of the huge variety of global farming types and products. Select a type of farming that you know little about, but are interested to find out more. Conduct some internet research, with the aim of producing a short PowerPoint® presentation (of no more than six slides) to describe your chosen farming type. Your PowerPoint® presentation should attempt to describe the characteristics and global locations of your chosen farm type. A good starting point is Wikipedia. There are some great photos at: www.aerialarchives.com/agriculture.htm

B   Where does my breakfast come from?

It is often said that breakfast is the most important meal of the day, as it sets you up for what lies ahead. Breakfast gives you the energy necessary to function effectively, just like a car needs petrol or diesel. What did you have for breakfast today? Do you know where your breakfast actually comes from (not just the local supermarket!)?

Look at Figure 3. It shows where in the world food items have come from, to make up a typical breakfast. Whilst some items such as flour for the bread (from wheat) and milk (from cows) come from nearby sources, several items have travelled a great distance to end up on the breakfast table. Even the homemade marmalade uses Seville oranges that come from Spain.

One reason for global sourcing of food is because some food crops grow best in warmer climates, such as oranges, pineapples and sugar cane. Another reason is that it can sometimes be cheaper to supply foods from elsewhere in the world, rather than from the UK.

▲ **Figure 4   A typical breakfast**

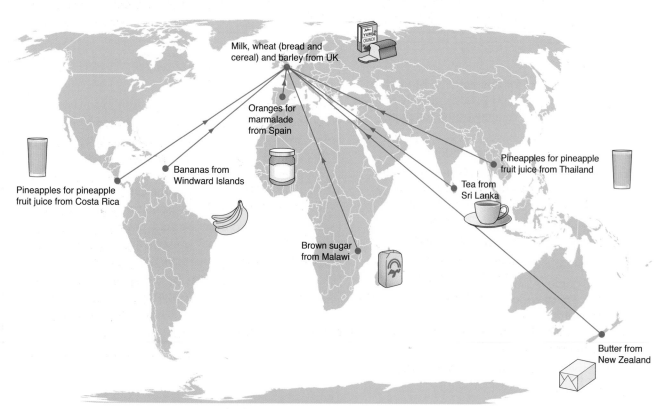

▲ **Figure 3   Where does my breakfast come from?**

The distance over which foods are transported is referred to as **food miles**. Some people are concerned that food is being transported further than necessary and that this is a waste of precious energy resources. In addition, by using large amounts of energy in transportation, we are adding needlessly to carbon emissions and global warming. Increasingly, there is a campaign in the UK and elsewhere in the world to 'eat locally', to support local farmers (Figure 4) and cut harmful carbon emissions.

Whilst the aim of reducing food miles is probably a good thing, it is not always the case that there is a direct link between distance and carbon emissions. For example, tomatoes grown outdoors in Spain and transported to the UK, can have a lower carbon emission than homegrown tomatoes grown in a heated greenhouse. The issue linking food miles to carbon emissions and global warming is a very complex one!

▲ **Figure 4   Farmer's market in Islington, London**

Activities

3 Study Figure 3.

 a) Use the atlas map on pages 136–37 to estimate the distance in miles that the food items have had to travel to the breakfast table in Bristol. Add the distances, to discover the overall 'breakfast food miles'.

 b) Which food item had to travel the furthest?

 c) Can you think why this food item had to come from so far away?

 d) Suggest a breakfast for yourself that would come entirely from food sources close to your home, say within about 50 miles. Try to present your answer in a similar style to that shown in Figure 3.

4 Study Figure 3. In this activity you are going to try to source as many food items as possible, for another meal of your choice. To do this, you are going to need to look closely at the packets and tins of food used to prepare a meal.

 a) Make a list of the ingredients and their source countries.

 b) Locate these countries on a blank world outline (using the atlas map on pages 136–37 to help you).

 c) Draw arrows linking each food source to your location in the UK.

 d) Use simple sketches or write the name of each food alongside the appropriate arrow.

 e) Complete your map by writing a title.

 f) Try to estimate the total food miles for your meal.

ICT ACTIVITY

The aim of this activity is to produce a poster. The poster is to make people aware of the issues surrounding food miles and to encourage them to 'buy local'. Think carefully about the foods that you feature, so that you really are promoting less energy use and trying to reduce carbon emissions. Avoid promoting foods that are grown very intensively in greenhouses, for example. Use your own artwork or illustrations from the Internet to make your poster colourful and interesting.

A good starting point is the BBC website at www.bbc.co.uk/food/food_matters/foodmiles.shtml

C Growing rice in the Ganges delta

Look back to Figure 3 on page 90. Notice that rice from China is used to make breakfast cereals, such as Kellogg's Special K. Rice is one of the most important food crops grown in the world. It is the main food crop for millions, particularly those living in countries like China, India, Bangladesh, Indonesia and the Philippines.

Rice is a **cereal crop** (a type of grass) so it is similar to cereals such as wheat, barley and oats that are grown in the UK. The reason that rice is not grown in the UK is because it requires constant high temperatures in excess of 21°C. It also needs to be submerged throughout its growing season in water to a depth of 2 to 3 centimetres. This explains why it is grown extensively on some of the world's largest river floodplains and deltas, such as the Ganges in India and Bangladesh, and the Yangtze in China. UK cereals are better suited to drier conditions.

The Ganges delta is a major rice-growing region (Figure 5). Its fertile soils and warm, wet climate provide ideal growing conditions. The rice takes between 100 and 150 days to grow, which means that it is possible to have two rice crops in a single year.

Most of the people living in this region are poor and they do not have access to machines. This means that they do many of the tasks by hand (Figure 6). Most of the farmers are **subsistence** farmers. This means that they concentrate on growing food for themselves and for their families. A small number of farmers in the area are wealthy and have large areas of land. They can afford to use expensive machines and chemical fertilisers to grow large amounts of rice for sale. These are **commercial** farmers. Look at Figure 7 to see the typical stages of rice growing in the Ganges delta.

▲ **Figure 5 Rice growing in the Ganges delta**

▲ **Figure 6 Rice planting by hand in the Ganges delta**

1 Preparation of land
The flat land is surrounded by low earth banks used to retain water when the land is flooded by 2 to 3 cm of water.

2 Ploughing
Land is ploughed and weeds removed.

3 Casting
Rice seedlings grown in a nurseryfield are transferred to the main fields and planted by hand.

4 Growing
Rice crop grows in the flooded field for 3 to 4 months.

5 Harvesting
The field is drained of water and when the rice plant turns brown the rice is harvested.

▲ **Figure 7 The stages of rice cultivation in the Ganges delta**

Activities

5 Study Figures 5 and 6.

a) Rice is used in a number of foods available in the UK. Apart from breakfast cereal, can you think of other uses of rice?

b) Why is the landscape shown in Figure 5 better suited to growing rice than other cereals (such as wheat and barley)?

c) What is happening in Figure 6?

d) Why is it possible to grow two, or even three, crops of rice in a single year?

e) Can you think of any problems that might result from growing so many crops of rice year after year?

f) What is the difference between a subsistence farmer and a commercial farmer?

g) Imagine that the farm in Figure 6 were to use machines, rather than hand labour. Consider the advantages and disadvantages of this change.

6 Study Figure 7.

a) Make a large copy of Figure 7. Use simple sketches or photos from the internet to illustrate your diagram.

b) Add another arrow to your diagram to show how rice cultivation is more or less a continuous cycle. Think carefully about which boxes to link together with your arrow.

c) Traditional rice cultivation can be described being **labour intensive**. What do you think is meant by this?

d) How might too much water create problems in growing rice?

ICT ACTIVITY

Extend your study of rice cultivation in the Ganges delta by accessing http://geographyfieldwork.com/RiceFarm.htm

• Draw a farm systems diagram to describe rice cultivation. Illustrate your diagram using simple sketches.

• What are the problems faced by rice farmers?

• Read about some of the recent changes that have affected rice farming. Choose three of these changes and write a few sentences about each one. Find a photo to illustrate each one.

D Fairtrade bananas from the Windward Islands

Look back to Figure 4 (page 90) and notice that the breakfast bananas came from the Windward Islands. The Windward Islands are a group of islands in the Caribbean comprising St Lucia, St Vincent and the Grenadines, Grenada and Dominica (Figure 8). Along with the majority of bananas now sold in UK supermarkets, the bananas in Figure 4 has a FAIRTRADE mark on it.

Fairtrade is an organisation that strives to provide farmers with a fair price for their produce (Figure 10) and to ensure that they get a better deal from world trade. In the past, farmers in poorer parts of the world received pitiful amounts of money for their produce, with most of the profits going to big businesses in the richer countries. Fairtrade is working to reduce these inequalities and help to maintain thriving rural communities in poorer countries.

Conrad James, banana farmer in St Lucia

Conrad James (Figure 9) has a small farm on the island of St Lucia. He has been selling his bananas into the Fairtrade market for several years. The tropical climate of St Lucia is ideal for growing bananas and each week Conrad harvests about a hundred 18 kg boxes of bananas. His three sons help him on his farm when they are not abroad working or studying. After harvesting, Conrad's bananas are loaded onto ships (Figure 11) to begin their long journey to supermarkets in the UK.

Bananas are crucial to the national economies of the Windward Islands. However, during the 1990s, competition from massive banana plantations in South America and Africa threatened to wipe out small-scale banana production in the Windward Islands, by flooding the market with cheap bananas. The number of banana farmers in the Windward Islands fell from 10,000 in 1990 to 1,800 in 2005.

Fairtrade Foundation has provided a lifeline for Conrad and other farmers like him by guaranteeing him a fair price.

By adding a premium payment of US$1.75 on each box of bananas, the Fairtrade Foundation has been able to fund improvements on farms and in rural parts of the Windward Islands. These include buying trimmers to help farmers control weeds, improving the quality of packing sheds, supporting education, building bus shelters and refurbishing community centres.

Conrad believes that Fairtrade has helped him and other small-scale farmers like him to survive. Without Fairtrade, he would almost certainly have been forced to abandon farming to get a job in industry, or even leave St Lucia to seek employment abroad.

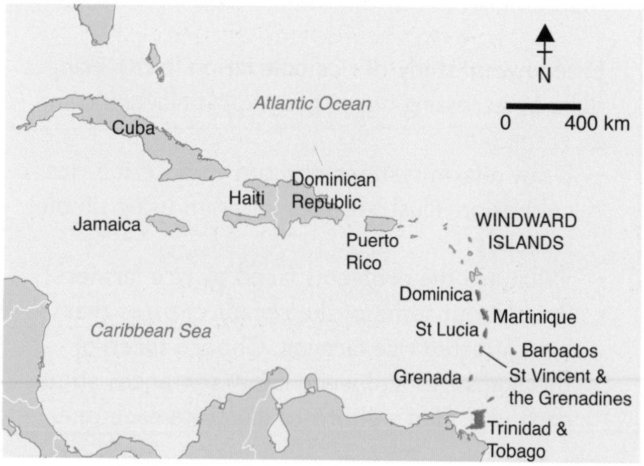

▲ Figure 8   Location of the Windward Islands in Caribbean

▲ Figure 9   Conrad James, Fairtrade banana farmer in St Lucia, Windward Islands

▲ **Figure 10   Fairtrade food products**

▲ **Figure 11   Fairtrade bananas being loaded onto ships**

Activities

7 Study Figure 10.

a) Make a list of the Fairtrade products shown in the photograph.

b) Do you and your family buy any Fairtrade products?

c) Are you aware of Fairtrade products being used in your school?

d) Why is it important to support small-scale farmers like Conrad James?

e) Some people think that the Fairtrade Foundation is maintaining high food costs and disadvantaging the consumer. Do you agree?

f) Do you think people should seek out Fairtrade products in a supermarket? Or should they go for the cheapest available (wherever and however it was produced)? Explain your answer.

8 For this activity you will need to work as a class (or in groups of four or five). The aim of the activity is to see where in the world Fairtrade products come from.

a) Produce a large wall display (based on a map of the world) to show the range of Fairtrade products available. You will need to work together to collect wrappings, labels and packaging from Fairtrade products. These will then need to be mounted on paper and positioned accurately on the world map.

b) Consider the global spread of Fairtrade products (globalisation). Are Fairtrade products concentrated in certain parts of the world? To what extent does the spread of Fairtrade define the poorer parts of the world? Is this another measure of development (see pages 13–14)?

RESEARCH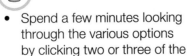

In this unit we have studied Fairtrade bananas. Now is your chance to make a similar study for a Fairtrade product of your choice.

- Access the Fairtrade website at www.fairtrade.org.uk and click 'Producers'.

- Spend a few minutes looking through the various options by clicking two or three of the products listed.
- Now make up your mind which one of the products you wish to study further.
- Write a short report (use an ICT package such as Publisher® or PowerPoint® if you wish) on your chosen product. Focus on an individual farmer if you can, and try to show how the farmer and the local community has benefited from being part of the Fairtrade Foundation.

E Food and famine in Africa

World food production has increased significantly in recent decades. This is due to improved technology, the use of fertilisers and pesticides, and the selective breeding of plants and animals. Wetlands have been drained and dry lands have been irrigated (Figure 12) to provide more and more land for food production. Yet despite all of these changes, millions of people, mainly in Africa, suffer from food shortages and even famine (Figure 13).

During the 20th century, some 70 million people died from famines worldwide. This is more than the entire current population of the UK. In the past, China was particularly badly affected by famines. Nowadays, it is Africa.

In Africa, food shortages and famine usually result from a combination of factors, rather than one single cause. Droughts are common in parts of Africa and can lead to overgrazing of the already fragile soils. This can in turn lead to severe soil erosion, resulting in poor harvests. In some countries, food production and distribution have been disrupted by wars. Elsewhere, good quality land may be used for growing cash crops for export, rather than producing food crops to satisfy local people. The situation is often highly complex.

Read through the information in Figure 14 to learn about the recent food shortages and threat of famine in the Darfur region of Sudan.

▲ **Figure 13   The famine in Sudan, 1998**

Activity

9 Study Figure 14.

Carry out a study into the food shortages in the Darfur region of Sudan. Use the information in Figure 14 together with additional Internet research. Your study should consider the following questions:

- Where are Sudan and the Darfur region?
- What is the physical geography and climate of the region?
- What are the causes of the recent food shortages? Read through the extracts to discover that there are both natural and human factors involved.
- Why are many people forced to leave the region?
- What do you think the future holds for the people of this region?

▲ **Figure 12   Irrigated farmland in the desert**

Where is Darfur?

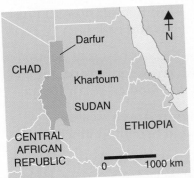

- more than 1.5 million displaced
- about 70,000 dead since February 2003
- more at risk from disease, starvation and lack of aid
- Arab militias accused of ethnic cleansing
- Sudan blames rebels for starting conflict

Darfur physical geography

Much of Darfur is dry, sandy desert (locally called *goz*) with gently rolling hills. There is little vegetation apart from some grass and low bushes. In the centre of the region is a range of volcanic peaks rising to over 3,000 metres. This is the only area where there is a permanent supply of water. Elsewhere, water has to be drawn from underground wells.

Darfur climate

For much of the year, Darfur is dry and hot. Rain falls during the rainy season from July to September. Rainfall is quite reliable in the south of the region (700 mm) but is far less reliable in the north, where drought conditions can occur.

Extract from the *Sudan Tribune*

The Darfur region of western Sudan is the site of the world's largest humanitarian operation. It is also on the verge of famine.

Humanitarians on the ground report an explosion in food prices – 500 per cent for cereals in one location – an ominous sign of famine. The UN World Food Programme also indicates that it is falling well short of pre-positioning adequate foodstocks prior to the rainy season, which coincides with the traditional 'hunger gap' between spring planting and fall harvest. Many locations in Darfur become completely inaccessible during the heavy rainy season, and food must be in place before **wadis** (dry river beds) become raging torrents, and the terrain a sea of mud.

Last autumn's harvests were disastrous, particularly in North and South Darfur (three-quarters of the region's population), and there is little evidence that future harvests will be better.

Khartoum's brutal Arab militia, the Janjaweed, keep African farmers from cultivating their lands through violent threats, and increasingly destroy crops before harvest.

Apple – Start

http://www.Rural communities face food shortages — Google

Buy Childre...uses Online   Quality Chil...ldingsDirect   Playhouses, ... playhouses   Mamas and P...t Kaboodle   Buy Mamas a... Shop for .   SCALLYWAGS ...ay Parties

Rural communities face food shortages

Thousands of people have died in Darfur, caught up in intense fighting between rebel groups and government troops. Over a million people have been forced from their homes.

Due to the conflict, villages have planted little food and many have had seeds, tools and livestock stolen. Without money to buy food and with little hope of successful harvests, food shortages seem inevitable.

Websites
http://news.bbc.co.uk/1/hi/world/africa/3754766.stm
http://sudanwatch.blogspot.com/2006/10/eyewitness-account-what-i-saw-in.html

▲ **Figure 14 Darfur famine**

F Issue: Should Kenyan farmers grow flowers for Europe?

If you know of someone who has received a rose on Valentine's Day, the chances are that it was grown in Kenya. After all, roses are not available in the UK in February! Kenya is famous for producing and exporting flowers to Europe, particularly during the winter, and it has become big business. Kenya earns over £80 million from exporting flowers each year, and this accounts for nearly 10 per cent of its export earnings.

Most flowers in Kenya are grown on the relatively fertile soils close to the lakes in the southwest of the country (Figure 15). Flower farming is an example of **intensive farming**, where expensive inputs result in high yields. Most flowers are grown inside greenhouses to create a perfect climatic. Expensive chemical fertilisers and pesticides are used to ensure that the plants are healthy. Many people work in the greenhouses to look after the flowers (Figure 16).

Despite the success of Kenya's flower industry, it has created problems and issues:

- Should some of Kenya's best soils be used to grow luxury cash crops for Europe, rather than much needed food crops for Kenya?

- Is it fair that a few relatively wealthy landowners should benefit so much?

- Is it fair that most of the workers are poorly paid and can be sacked at any time, including women who fall pregnant?

- Should precious water supplies be diverted away from other people's farmland in order to supply the flower industry?

- There are some indications that chemicals used in the flower industry are polluting water sources.

- Should UK supermarkets continue to buy Kenyan flowers? Should they only buy Fairtrade flowers?

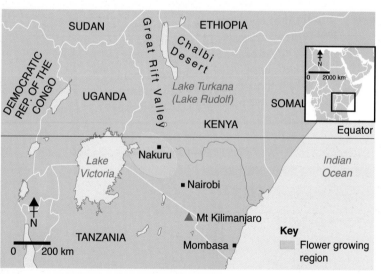

▲ **Figure 15   Kenya**

▲ **Figure 16   People working on a flower farm in Kenya**

RESEARCH

Consider the issue of flower growing in Kenya.

- Use the information in this unit (together with the websites listed below) to help you identify the advantages and disadvantages of flower growing in Kenya. Who are the winners and losers? Conduct additional Internet research if you wish. You should consider the economy of the country, the landowners, the workers and the local farmers.

- Find out about Fairtrade flowers by accessing the websites listed below. What are the advantages of Fairtrade flowers for the producers and consumers? Are there any disadvantages?

- Do you think UK supermarkets should only purchase Fairtrade flowers from Kenya? Why?

www.learningafrica.org.uk/downloads/casestudy_flowers.pdf

www.guardian.co.uk/uk/2006/oct/21/kenya.world

www.globaleye.org.uk/secondary_autumn05/eyeon/flowerpower.html

www.fairtrade.org.uk/producers/flowers/finlay_flowers_oserian_ravine_roses_kenya.aspx

Managing Resources

8

A What are resources?

The word 'resource' is quite difficult to define in a single sentence. It refers to an aspect of the environment, either natural or artificial, that is needed by people or has a use.

Look at Figures 1 and 2, which show several resources. Figure 1 show a quarry where limestone is being extracted from the ground. Limestone is an important resource that is used to make cement. It is also used as **aggregate** (broken rock fragments) in making roads. When crushed into powder, it is spread onto fields to reduce the acidity of the soil. There are also some less obvious resources shown in Figure 1. These include the energy used to power the machines, and the people themselves whose knowledge and skills form an important human resource. The landscape too is a resource, providing beauty and artistic inspiration, as much as land for farming, forestry and recreation.

Many of the world's resources are limited and need to be managed in a sustainable way if they are to be available to future generations. Without careful management, some resources will decline in their quality or become too expensive to obtain. Others may quite simply run out. Thoughtless use of resources can have harmful effects on the environment, causing pollution of the atmosphere or contamination of water supplies. Look at Figure 3 on page 100 to see some of the recent issues involving the world's resources.

▲ Figure 1 Limestone quarrying in Yorkshire

Activity

1 Work with a friend for this activity. Study Figure 2.

   a) Look carefully at the photograph and make a list of as many resources as possible. Try to include naturally available resources as well as human or man-made resources.

   b) Now select two colours, one to represent natural resources and the other man-made resources. Work through your list using the appropriate colour to underline each resource.

   c) Which of the resources in your list need careful management and why?

   d) If the resources shown in Figure 2 were not carefully managed, how might this photograph look different in ten years' time?

▲ Figure 2 Coastal landscape on a Greek island

Activity

2 Study Figure 3. The aim of this activity is to produce a poster collage to identify some recent issues associated with global resources. Use the information in Figure 3 to get you started, together with the internet. Try to identify some issues that have arisen since the publication of this book, by accessing news sites such as the BBC. Present your poster collage on a single sheet of paper and display in your classroom. Use your initiative with illustrations, using materials, wrappers and other items, to bring your poster to life.

ICT ACTIVITY

The aim of this activity is to create an annotated photograph to identify a selection of resources and some possible issues associated with them.

- Firstly, you need to select a photograph similar to Figures 1 and 2 on page 99. Both show a variety of resources. To do this you need to think of an environment, such as a coast, and then try to narrow down your Google™ search, e.g. 'Spain coast photo'.
- Once you have selected your photo, copy and paste it onto a Word® document and centre it.
- Now add text boxes and arrows to identify a selection of resources. For each one, consider an issue associated with it. For example, a fishing boat may cause a reduction in fish stocks by over-fishing or pollution of the water.
- Complete your work by writing a title.
- Print out your annotated photo and display in your classroom.

Air pollution and greenhouse gas emissions from coal fired power stations and heavy industry

Pollution of water results from intensive farming and the widespread use of chemicals

Over-fishing is reducing fish stocks in some parts of the world

Deforestation and burning of forests contribute to the greenhouse effect and can lead to soil erosion

Will oil and gas run out before new sources of energy can be found?

Water is becoming a scarce resource in many parts of the world. Some politicians are predicting 'water wars' in the future

Should whales be hunted or protected?

The world's deserts are spreading as a result of overgrazing and overcultivation in semi-desert areas

Through lack of education some people are unable to develop skills and ideas necessary to make the most of their human resources

Coral reefs (important habitats for fish) are being damaged by pollution, tourism and climate change

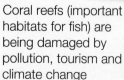

▲ **Figure 3 Global resource issues**

B Water: the world's most precious resource?

Water is a vital resource that supports all forms of life on the Earth. Not only is it necessary for drinking, but it also supports farming, industry, and the production of power. Without water, the Earth would be a dead planet.

In the UK, we are fortunate in have plentiful supplies of water. Any water shortages that we suffer tend to be short lived. However, elsewhere in the world, water is a very precious resource that needs to be harvested, stored and conserved (Figure 5). An estimated 2 billion people, in over 60 countries, do not have access to the recognised minimum requirement of 50 litres a day for drinking, bathing, cooking and sanitation. Poor water management can be disastrous to the natural environment and the communities that live there (Figure 6).

▲ **Figure 5 Water: a precious resource**

Activity

3 Study Figures 5 and 6.

a) Draw a spider diagram to show the variety of uses for water. Draw a central box with 'WATER' written in it, and then write the uses of water around the central box. Use simple sketches or diagrams to illustrate each use you have identified.

b) Draw a pie graph to show how the basic water requirement of 50 litres per person per day is used (Figure 4). To convert the figures (out of 50) to degrees (out of 360) you should multiply by 7.2. Explain what each segment represents and write a title.

c) What is the evidence in Figure 6 that water has been mismanaged in this environment?

Purpose	Litres (per person per day)
Drinking	5
Sanitation	20
Bathing	15
Cooking	10
Total	**50**

▲ **Figure 4 Recommended minimum water requirement**

▲ **Figure 6 Bad water management**

Water supply and storage

You have probably learned about the **water cycle** in science (Figure 7). It describes the processes involved in the constant recycling of water between the Earth and the atmosphere. Understanding the water cycle is important in being able to identify potential sources of water.

Most of the world's freshwater comes from surface **reservoirs** or rivers. Many of the world's rivers have artificial dams, which create reservoirs to store water (Figure 8). Once stored, the water can be released slowly to provide irrigation for crops, as well as freshwater for drinking. By controlling river flow, dams help to reduce the threat of flooding. In maintaining a steady flow and river level, they also make river transport safer and more reliable. Reservoirs provide opportunities for catching fish, which is a very important source of protein in many parts of the world. Many modern dams, such as the Three Gorges Project (Figure 8), also produce **hydro-electric power**, which is an important renewable source of energy.

In places where the underlying rocks are **porous** (contain holes), underground reservoirs or **aquifers** are formed. Water can be piped to the surface through boreholes sunk deep into the rocks below. Aquifers supply many of the major cities of the world including London, Mexico City and Los Angeles.

Activity

4 Study Figure 7.
  a) Make a large and colourful copy of the water cycle diagram.
  b) Locate and label the following features associated with water supply:
     - dam
     - reservoir
     - river
     - aquifer
     - desalination plant
  c) Why is the term 'cycle' used to describe what happens to water?
  d) Why is an understanding of the water cycle important for water engineers, whose job it is to provide a secure water supply to an area?
  e) Why is it important to balance supply and demand in water management?

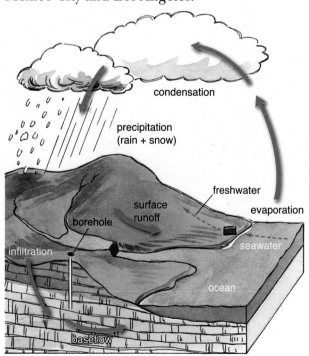

▲ Figure 7 The water cycle

▲ Figure 8 The Three Gorges Project, China

In desert regions, for example in Egypt and Jordan, underground aquifers provide much needed water to support farming and settlements (Figure 9). However, these aquifers are 'fossil' aquifers and were created thousands of years ago when the climate in the region was much wetter than it is today. Today, the rate of water pumping exceeds the natural recharge by rainfall. This is unsustainable, and means that this source of water could eventually run out.

In particularly dry coastal regions, desalination plants convert seawater into freshwater using complex and very expensive chemical processes. This happens in countries such as Saudi Arabia and the United Arab Emirates.

A much cheaper and highly imaginative method of '**water harvesting**' is used in the Atacama Desert in Chile. Here a system of harvesting nets is used to collect water droplets from the frequent fogs that shroud this remote and dry region. The droplets run down the wires to be collected in pipes and vessels at the bottom (Figure 10).

RESEARCH

1   Use the internet to produce a factsheet describing the 'Three Gorges Project' in China. Your factsheet should contain information about the following aspects:

    •   the location of The Three Gorges project in China

    •   a brief history and description of the scheme

    •   advantages of the scheme

    •   disadvantages of the scheme.

    Include maps (preferably hand drawn) and photographs.

2   Carry out a short project looking at 'Water supply in the Desert'. People who live in desert regions have to cope with a serious lack of water. They need to manage water very carefully if it is to be a sustainable resource. Find out more about the use of aquifers, desalination plants and water harvesting techniques, using carefully worded internet searches. Present your report electronically using PowerPoint®.

▲ Figure 10   Water harvesting in Chile

▲ Figure 9   Intensive cultivation of tomatoes using irrigation near As Safawi, Jordan

C Global energy resources

Energy is needed to provide heat and power for our homes, for industry and for transport. There is a huge range of energy sources in the world, including wood, coal, oil, gas, wind and geothermal. In Book 1 we studied wind power, and in Book 2 we looked at solar energy.

It is possible to sort energy sources into two groups, renewable (can be used continuously without running out) and non-renewable or fossil (limited and will eventually run out). Winds, solar, waves and geothermal are examples of renewable energy whereas coal, oil and gas are examples of non-renewable energy.

Energy resources are not distributed evenly across the world. Look at Figure 11. It shows the global energy balance. Notice that some regions produce more energy than they use (energy surplus) whereas others consume more than they produce (energy deficit). To restore the balance, energy is traded and shipped around the world using huge super tankers and pipelines (Figure 12).

▲ **Figure 12   Oil pipelines transporting oil in Russia**

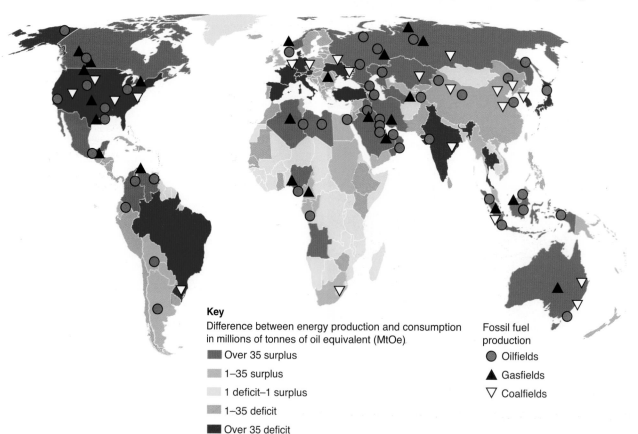

Key

Difference between energy production and consumption in millions of tonnes of oil equivalent (MtOe)

- Over 35 surplus
- 1–35 surplus
- 1 deficit–1 surplus
- 1–35 deficit
- Over 35 deficit

Fossil fuel production

- ● Oilfields
- ▲ Gasfields
- ▽ Coalfields

▲ **Figure 11   Global energy balance**

Hydro-electric power – the global fuel of the future?

Hydro-electric power (HEP) is an example of renewable energy. It uses flowing water to generate electricity (Figure 13). In most cases, dams are used to create reservoirs such as the Three Gorges Project in China (Figure 8, page 102). The level of the water stored behind the dam is raised, and this creates a head of water between the reservoir and the valley below. When water passes through pipes in the dam, it does so at speed and is therefore able to generate electricity by turning the turbine (Figure 13).

Look at Figure 14 on page 106. Notice that hydro-electric power (HEP) provides electricity in many countries throughout the world. For the future, HEP has the potential to provide the world with a great deal of energy, particularly if countries work together to establish international electricity grids, so that electricity can be transmitted between countries.

One of the great attractions of hydro-electric power is that it is non-polluting, and the same water can be used to generate electricity several times throughout a river's course. However, as you will have discovered with your research into China's Three Gorges Project, hydro-electric power does have some disadvantages, especially when land has to be flooded to create reservoirs.

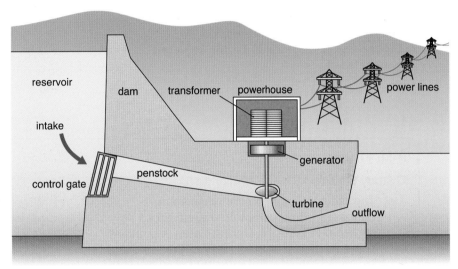

▲ **Figure 13 Inside a hydroelectric power station**

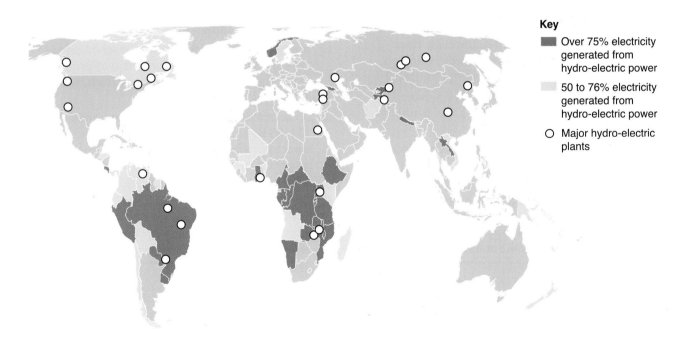

Key

■ Over 75% electricity generated from hydro-electric power

□ 50 to 76% electricity generated from hydro-electric power

○ Major hydro-electric plants

▲ **Figure 14 Electricity generation from hydro-electric power (2004)**

Surplus (over 35)	Surplus (1–35)	Balance	Deficit (1–35)	Deficit (over 35)
India	Japan	Brazil	Australia	China
Canada	France	USA	Argentina	Indonesia
Kenya	Saudi Arabia	Russia	Nigeria	
			Norway	
			Venezuela	

NB Values in millions of tonnes of oil equivalent (MtOe)

▲ **Figure 15   Energy balance for selected countries**

RESEARCH

Produce a single-side report on one of the hydro-electricity power stations identified in Figure 14. Your report should include the following:

*   map showing its location
*   photograph of the hydro-electricity power plant
*   reasons why the location was chosen for a power plant
*   advantages and disadvantages of the scheme

Use a Google™ search to look up two or three possible options and then select one that interests you and that enables you to address the aspects listed above.

Activities

5   Study Figures 11 (page 104) and 15.

   a)   The table in Figure 15 identifies some countries with different energy balances as shown on Figure 11. Unfortunately it contains some mistakes! Make a copy of the table and re-arrange the countries so that they are in the correct columns.

   b)   How does Figure 11 suggest that energy is moved around the world between countries?

   c)   Use Figure 12 (page 104) to describe how energy is moved around the world. Can you think of any other forms of energy transfer?

   d)   Locate the USA. Despite having an overall energy deficit, what fossil fuels are produced in the country?

   e)   Russia is a major exporter of gas. Use Figure 11 to suggest where you think most of the gas goes. Explain your answer.

   f)   Brazil and India have a serious energy deficit. They have limited amounts of fossil fuels. What do you suggest they do to increase their energy production without having to rely on other countries?

6   Study Figures 13 and 14 (page 105).

   a)   Why is hydro-electricity an example of a renewable form of energy?

   b)   Describe with the aid of a simple diagram how flowing water can be used to generate electricity.

   c)   What are the advantages and disadvantages of hydro-electricity? Present your answer in the form of a table.

   d)   Study Figure 14. Use the atlas map on pages 136–37 to identify five countries that produce more than 75 per cent electricity from hydro-electricity.

   e)   Look at the physical atlas map on pages 134–35 to see whether all or most of the selected hydro-electricity plants are located in mountain areas. Give some examples in your answer.

   f)   Consider energy supply in Brazil. By referring to Figures 11 and 14 as well as the physical atlas map, can you suggest why Brazil produces a great deal of electricity from hydro-electricity?

D Human resources and the fashion industry

The fashion industry illustrates the value of human resources (Figure 16). There are a great many positive aspects of the fashion industry, such as its inventiveness and imagination. Millions of people work in the global fashion industry, in factories making clothes, in distribution, in advertising, and in retailing. Imagine a high street without its fashion shops!

However, in some cases, factory workers in poorer countries have been exploited in order to keep manufacturing costs as low as possible and boost profits. By paying low wages, retailers can buy products cheaply and sell them competitively.

In February 2009, London Fashion Week opened amid controversy following reports than some of the UK's leading fashion retailers were buying clothes made by poorly paid workers in 'sweatshops' around the world.

● The charity War on Want identified Bangladeshi workers as earning as little as 7p an hour making fashion clothes for Primark, Tesco and Asda.

● Migrant workers (some of whom were illegal immigrants) were discovered working in a Manchester factory for 12 hours a day, 7 days a week for just £3 an hour, well below the minimum wage in the UK.

● In 2008, the *Guardian* reported on Indian workers (Figure 18, page 108) producing clothes for Gap's upmarket chain Banana Republic, working for up to 70 hours a week for less than an acceptable '**living wage**' (that required to pay for housing, food and healthcare).

Charities such as War on Want and Oxfam, together with ethical fashion organisations, are seeking to establish codes of conduct to ensure that people working in the fashion industry earn a reasonable living wage and work in reasonable conditions. One organisation called 'Ethical Fashion Forum' works with fashion retailers to raise standards by promoting sustainability and fair treatment for its workers.

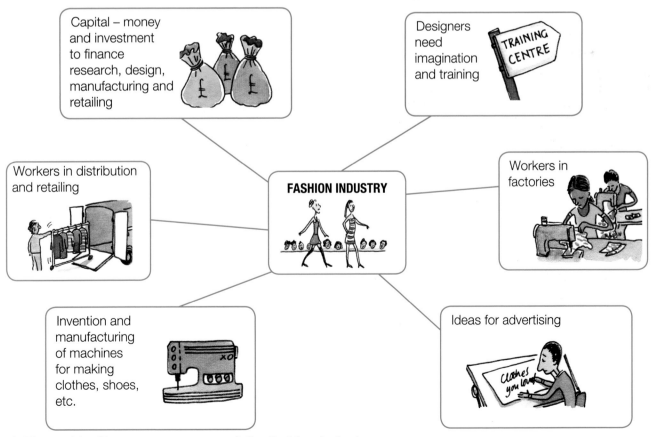

▲ **Figure 16 Human resources and the fashion industry**

▲ **Figure 17 Women workers in a garment factory in India**

RESEARCH

One well-known fashion company that has received a good deal of negative publicity in recent years is the sportswear giant Nike. Recent reports have suggested that some shoes and clothes have been manufactured in 'sweatshops', poor quality factories where people work long hours for low wages. The aim of this research activity is for you to find out more about these accusations and decide whether you think they are true.

For this activity you should work in pairs. You must recognise that a lot of the sites you may visit on the internet present one side of the debate. It is important that you try to find out what Nike have to say and also that you refer to some impartial websites, such as world media organisations like the BBC.

Present your findings in the form of a PowerPoint® presentation. This issue could then be debated in class. Should teenagers like you continue to buy Nike products?

Activities

7 This is a whole class activity and involves some preparation at home. It is an excellent illustration of globalisation (see page 9).

   a) Take a look through your wardrobe at the labels of clothes, shoes and other fashion items. Complete a table identifying the clothing or fashion item and the country where it was made.

   b) As a class, share the information and produce a master table to see which countries are involved in making most of the clothes and other fashion items that your class buys.

   c) Present this information in the form of a flow map, using flow lines of different thickness to represent the number of items made. Use the flow lines to connect the countries of origin to the UK.

   d) Comment on the results of your class study. Are most fashion items made in poor countries?

8 Study Figure 17.

   a) What do you think it would be like to work in the factory in the photo?

   b) Why do some companies choose to have their clothes made in countries such as India and Bangladesh?

   c) Why do you think the workers are all women?

   d) What is the 'living wage'?

   e) Do you think the 'living wage' should be extended to cover other living expenses? What else do you think should be covered?

   f) If companies are forced to increase workers' wages what problem could result?

   g) Why do you think some of the people working in the Manchester factory were illegal immigrants?

   h) How can the public put pressure on companies not to use cheap labour in making their clothes?

   i) Figure 16 (page 107) identifies a number of human resources involved in the fashion industry. Can you think of any others?

E Global fishing industry

For some people, 'fish'n'chips' is the national UK dish (Figure 18). The choice of fish is, however, usually restricted to cod, haddock and plaice, all of which are sourced close to the UK in the northern North Sea. If you were to visit the fish counter in your local supermarket you would find a much greater variety of fish from all over the world, including salmon, herring, bass, shrimp, lobster and tuna.

Look at Figure 19 to see the world's major fishing grounds. Notice that commercial fishing grounds exist off almost all coastal waters around the world. China is the top producer of fish, followed by Peru and Japan. Over 90 million tonnes of fish are caught annually across the world. Commercial fishing involves wild fish, caught in open waters, together with farmed fish, such as salmon and shrimp. These fish are usually kept in netted compounds and farmed intensively in shallow coastal or inland waters.

One important factor affecting the location of fishing grounds is the presence of cold **ocean currents**. These are usually associated with the upwelling of deep cold water, which brings plentiful supplies of nutrients to the surface for fish to feed on.

▲ Figure 18   Eating 'fish 'n' chips'

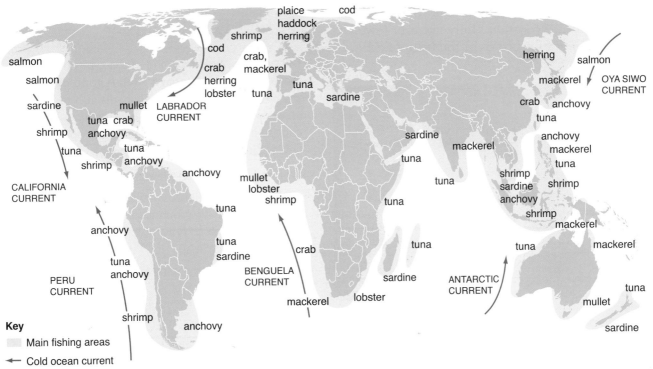
▲ Figure 19   Major global fishing grounds

The fishing industry worldwide is very important. Many people are employed as fishermen and others work in fish processing factories (Figure 20). Boats have to be built and maintained and all the specialist equipment made. Fishing brings in a large amount of money to countries and the fish provides a valuable source of protein for people.

▲ **Figure 20 Fish processing factory in Canada**

One of the main issues facing the fishing industry involves **overfishing**. This is where fish stocks in certain areas have been harvested at a greater rate than the natural rate of fish replacement. The problem has been made worse by the use of fine-mesh nets that catch all fish big and small (Figure 21). The smaller, younger fish are either discarded or used for other purposes such as making fertiliser. With the younger fish removed from the system, there are ever fewer fish to become fully-grown in the future and stocks decline.

▲ **Figure 21 Fish catch in Mexico**

Activities

9   Study Figure 19 on page 109.

   a)   Apart from plaice, cod and mackerel, which other fish can be caught close to the UK?

   b)   Why do you think the world's major fishing grounds are almost all bordering land? (See if you can think of one human factor and one factor to do with fish!)

   c)   Why are many of the world's major fishing grounds close to cold ocean currents?

   d)   Anchovies are often used as a pizza topping. Where in the world do they come from?

   e)   In Alaskan restaurants, one type of fish dominates over all others. Which one?

   f)   What is 'fish farming'? What do you think are some of the advantages of fish farming?

10   Study Figures 20 and 21.

   a)   Make a list of the different jobs associated with the fishing industry.

   b)   Apart from providing many opportunities for employment, what are the other advantages of the fishing industry?

   c)   What do you think is happening in Figure 21.

   d)   Why is Figure 21 showing unsustainable fishing?

   e)   What do you think should be done to conserve fish stocks and ensure that they become sustainable?

RESEARCH

Carry out a study into one of the types of fish located in Figure 19 (page 109). A good overview with many useful links is Wikipedia at http://en.wikipedia.org/wiki/Commercial_fishing. You could choose a wild fish or a farmed fish. Produce your findings in the form of a short report.

Your study should include the following aspects:

*   Draw a fully labelled map to show the location of the main fishing grounds for your chosen fish. Use a photograph or drawing of your chosen fish to illustrate your map.

*   Write some interesting facts about your chosen fish, including how it is caught and what it is used for. Is it processed? Where is it exported? Is it a valuable source of income where it is caught?

*   Are fish stocks being sustainably managed? Are there any issues of interest?

F   Issue: Should whaling be completely banned?

One of today's most controversial fishing issues concerns the catching of whales, or **whaling**, as it is known. Dating back to at least 6000 BC, whaling is an ancient form of fishing that used to involve large fleets of boats to track down and hunt whales. In the early days, whales provided an important source of fuel oil as well as meat.

Nowadays, whaling is mostly for meat and involves only a small number of countries, with Norway and Japan being the top two producers of whale meat in the world. Modern whaling involves the use of giant factory ships to catch and process the whales (Figure 22). This is necessary because whales are often caught in open water a long way from processing factories on land.

Whaling is hugely controversial for a number of reasons. In the past, over-fishing of whales threatened their survival and there were concerns that some species may be hunted to extinction. Whales are considered to be intelligent animals and are thought to suffer considerably while being hunted and caught.

In 1986, in response to these and other concerns, the International Whaling Commission introduced a ban on whaling. Whilst most countries welcomed the ban, some objected to it and have continued whaling. Instead, they have set their own limits or **quotas**. Norway, for example, has a quota of just over 1,000 minke whales (although only about half the quota is actually caught).

Having ceased whaling in 1989, Iceland controversially started whaling again in 2006, setting itself a quota of 30 minke whales, out of an estimated total of 174,000 animals in the North Atlantic.

Should these and other countries be allowed to continue whaling or should it be totally banned?

▼ **Figure 22   Whale meat being processed**

Activity

11 The aim of this activity is for you to have a class debate to decide if you think whaling should be banned across the world. In order to have an informed discussion, you need to conduct your own research to discover both sides of the argument. You need to find out why so many countries have stopped whaling and wish to see it banned in others. You also need to understand why some countries, such as Norway, Japan and Iceland, wish to continue whaling. Are people's concerns genuine or is some limited whaling perfectly sustainable? Once you have completed your own study, you can then hold an informed class debate on the issue.

- A good starting point to give you an overview is Wikipedia at http://en.wikipedia.org/wiki/Whaling.

- To find out about some of the arguments against whaling, conservation groups such as Greenpeace www.greenpeace.org/international/campaigns/oceans/whaling and WWF www.wwf.org.uk/what_we_do/safeguarding_the_natural_world/wildlife/whales provide plenty of information.

- To read about some of the arguments in favour of whaling, access links at www.fishingsociety.org/ProWhalingSites.html.

- The BBC has excellent objective articles on the issue such as http://news.bbc.co.uk/1/hi/sci/tech/8042713.stm.

Tourism

9

A Global tourism: patterns and trends

Today, tourism is one of the world's most important industries, generating wealth and employment opportunities in almost every corner of the world. In 2007, there were over 900 million international tourist arrivals around the world. This number does not include all those people taking a holiday in their own country. Several countries (such as Greece,

Thailand and Namibia) rely heavily on tourism to support their economies. In the UK, tourism is worth over £60 billion a year, which is equivalent to about 5 per cent of the country's total income.

Look at the map of tourism in Figure 1. It looks rather weird, because it is a different view or **projection** than we are used to seeing. Notice that

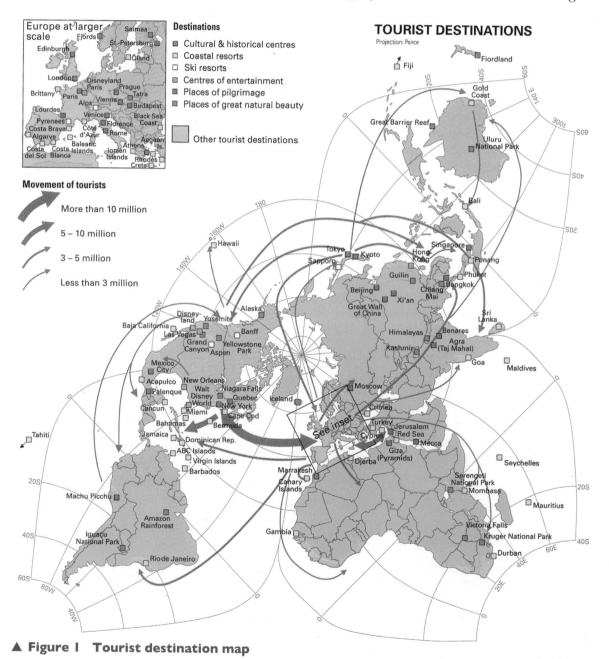

▲ **Figure 1   Tourist destination map**

there is a great range of tourist attractions indicated by the symbols. Are there any places that you have visited? Look at the purple arrows. These are **flow lines** and they indicate the number of tourists following popular routes from one country to another.

Tourism has grown rapidly in the last few decades. The cost of air travel has fallen with the introduction of 'budget' airlines, such as easyJet and Ryanair. What was once a luxury form of transport only available to the very wealthy is now accessible to most people as an alternative to rail and road. In many countries such as the UK, people are generally wealthier and have more disposable income to spend on extras such as holidays. People are also living longer and have more free time than in the past.

Whilst tourism brings many benefits, such as extra income and employment (Figure 2) it can also introduce a number of disadvantages (Figure 3). Natural environments can become damaged by intense human pressure and they can also become polluted. Jobs tend to be poorly paid, low status and seasonal in nature. Tourists from rich countries, who bring with them issues of drugs, alcohol and sex tourism, can affect local customs and cultures negatively. It is all about striking a balance, which is why tourism today strives to be sustainable.

▲ **Figure 2   The advantages of tourism**

▲ **Figure 3   The disadvantages of tourism**

Activities

1 Study Figure 1.

   a) Name a 'cultural and historical centre' in Europe (but not in the UK).

   b) Name a place of 'great natural beauty' in Australia.

   c) How many places of 'great natural beauty' have been identified in Africa?

   d) Name a 'place of pilgrimage' outside Europe. In which country is it located?

   e) How many tourists travel between the USA and Europe?

   f) How many people travel from the USA to the Caribbean?

   g) Which Indonesian coastal resort is particularly popular with Australians?

   h) Goa in India is a popular destination for travellers from Europe. How many people visit Goa?

   i) In which countries are the following attractions:

- Kruger National Park
- Iguaca National Park
- Great Wall of China (!)
- Grand Canyon
- Taj Mahal
- Fiordland

2 You need to work in pairs for this activity. Study Figure 3.

   a) Look carefully at the scenes in Figure 3 and make a list of some of the disadvantages and problems associated with tourism. Some are very obvious, but others will require a bit of thought. Consider the social (people), economic (money) and environmental impacts of your observations on the local area and beyond.

   b) Do you think the areas shown in the photos will continue to be popular with tourists in the future? Explain your answer.

   c) Suggest ways of addressing some of the problems you have identified. How could the resorts become more sustainable in the future?

B Tourism in America's 'sunshine state'

Florida (Figure 4) is one of the most popular destinations for tourists in the USA. Blessed with long hours of sunshine and warm temperatures throughout the year, it is a welcome winter escape for both Americans and Europeans. Some 60 million people visit the state each year (which is equivalent to the entire population of the UK).

Most Europeans who visit Florida head for Orlando and the theme parks (Figure 5). Nearly 50 million people visit the theme parks each year. The Walt Disney World Resort, comprising four separate theme parks, is the largest holiday resort in the world. Other theme park resorts in the Orlando area include Universal Orlando Resort and SeaWorld. Have you visited any of these theme parks?

Unlike many of the theme parks in Europe, the Orlando area benefits from having a huge amount of space on which to build. This means that, despite the massive theme parks and the large number of visitors, there are still wide-open spaces of countryside between the roads, hotels and other developments.

Over 50,000 people are employed in Orlando's industries, many of which are connected in some way to (or benefit from) the nearby theme parks and the international airport. The high-tech nature of Orlando's theme parks has led to the city becoming a centre for industrial computer-driven innovation and research, with many digital industries choosing to locate there. It is also a base for military simulation and training, film, television and electronic gaming.

▲ **Figure 5** **Orlando theme parks**

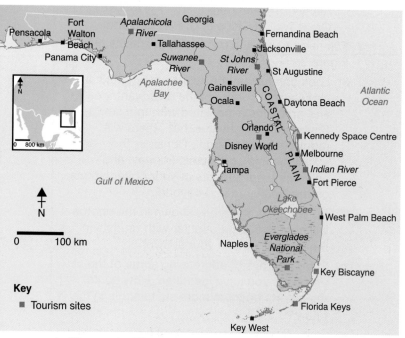

▲ **Figure 4 Florida: America's sunshine state**

Key
■ Tourism sites

Activities

3 Study Figure 4.

   a) Use the scale to work out the distance from Jacksonville in the north of Florida to Key West in the south.

   b) Is the coast of Florida mainly lowland or hills?

   c) How does your answer to (b) above help to explain why Florida's coast has been so extensively developed for tourism?

   d) Apart from the Orlando theme parks, can you suggest some other attractions for tourists in Florida? Use the internet to help.

4 Study Figure 5.

   a) Study Figure 5. Do you think this is a good site for a theme park? Why?

   b) How have Orlando's theme parks had a positive spin-off effect on the growth of industry in the city?

Elsewhere in the state, southern Florida offers several environmental attractions (Figure 4). The Everglades National Park is a wetlands wilderness famous for its diverse wildlife including bears, panthers and alligators.

At the southernmost tip of the state is Florida Keys, a string of low-lying coral limestone islands joined together by a causeway road that runs all the way to Key West. With its nearby coral reef, the Keys are a popular fishing, diving and snorkelling destination (Figure 6). There are a great many employment opportunities in the many small harbours and marinas as well as in hotels, gift shops and restaurants.

▲ **Figure 6   Tourism in Florida Keys**

 ICT ACTIVITY

Imagine that you work for a local travel agent. You have just received a number of emails asking you for information about tourism in Florida (Figure 7). Start by selecting just three of the questions in Figure 7 and use the internet to find the answers. Do not spend more than ten minutes on each one (your boss says, 'Time is money!'). In your reply, you can include one image (map or photo) and you should give some useful websites too.

Activity

5 Study Figure 6.

a) Study Figure 4. Use the scale to work out the length of the Florida Keys by measuring the distance between Key Largo and Key West.

b) Assuming an average speed of 30 mph, how long would it take you to drive from one end of the Keys to the other?

c) Why do you think Florida Keys is popular with tourists?

d) How do local people benefit from tourists visiting the Florida Keys?

e) For a bonus mark, see if you can find out the name of the famous author who lived in Key West. What was his best-known book?

Inbox	
From	**Message**
Sheila Moos	Hi, can you please tell me what weather I can expect in Miami in April? Thanks.
B. Redd	Hello, can you tell me what the attractions are at the Kennedy Space Centre, when it is open and how much it costs? Cheers.
Monty Stand	Hey, I have heard that it is worth visiting the Art Deco area of Miami. Can you tell me where it is and what there is to see? Thanks.
Mollie	Hi, I really want to see some manatees. Can you tell me where I should go in Florida to see some? Thank you.
B.B. Duck	Hello, I am booked in to a hotel in Marathon in the Keys. What is there to see and do in the town?
I. Freehly	Hi, I am staying with friends in Jacksonville and thought about visiting Amelia Island. Can you tell me what there is to see on the island? LOL! Thanks.
Elspeth Goate	Hi, I am staying with some university friends in Gainesville and would like to do some walks or bike rides while I am there. Are there any good bike trails or parks with walking trails? Thanks.

▲ **Figure 7   Emails requiring tourist information about Florida**

C Namibia: tourism on the wild side

Namibia is a country in southern Africa (Figure 8) that is well known for its wonderfully contrasting landscapes. Just inland from the coast is the Namib Desert, which is believed to be the oldest desert in the world. To the east is a high range of volcanic mountains rising to over 2,400 m. Deep canyons have been cut into the landscape where the mountains meet the lowland plains. In recent years, Namibia has become a popular destination for **adventure tourism**.

Adventure tourism involves activities that are more physical and potentially riskier than standard beach or city-based tourism. It can include wildlife safaris, walking trips, diving and kayaking. With its wild desert landscapes, deep canyons and spectacular mountains, Namibia offers a great many opportunities for adventure tourism (Figure 9).

Tourism is extremely important to the economy of Namibia. About one million people travel to Namibia each year, mostly from South Africa, Germany and the UK. Tourism provides a great many employment opportunities for local people, who can act as guides and instructors and work in hotels and restaurants. As tourism becomes developed, local people can also work

▲ **Figure 8   Map of Namibia**

in the construction industry: improving roads and building hotels and visitor centres. Tourists provide a market for local produce, including arts and crafts.

Walvis Bay is the second biggest town in Namibia. It is situated between two extreme landscapes, with the world's oldest desert (the Namib Desert) on one side and a massive lagoon on the other. It is a centre for activity holidays offering shark angling, sea kayaking and kite surfing, 4 X 4 desert safaris, dune hang gliding, dune surfing and quad biking. It offers opportunities

to see extensive marine and desert wildlife as well as ancient historic monuments.

Etosha is one of several National Parks in Namibia. The Park is dominated

by a huge salt pan (dried up desert lake) that fills with water for a few weeks each summer attracting many birds, such as pelicans and flamingos. Despite the extreme conditions, the area has abundant wildlife including the endangered black rhino. Safaris are popular within Etosha although there are strict controls to preserve the natural environment.

There are several spectacular canyons where the mountains meet the Namib Desert, such as the **Kuiseb Canyon** (Figure 10, page 117). These canyons are largely unexplored and, with temperatures over 50 °C and a lack of water, they are extremely hostile environments. In the future they may become destinations for extreme tourism.

▲ **Figure 9   Opportunities and attractions for adventure tourism in Namibia**

Activity

6 Study Figure 10.

a) Locate Windhoek, the capital of Namibia. Most international travellers arrive at the nearby international airport. Describe how tourists could travel on to have a holiday at Walvis Bay.

b) What are the opportunities and tourist facilities on offer in the Walvis Bay area?

c) Locate the C14 road running east from Walvis Bay. Follow this road until you reach Kuiseb Pass. Why might you stop here for a photograph?

d) What form of accommodation is available at Kuiseb Pass?

e) Describe the route that would take you on a circular tour from Kuiseb Pass through Nauchas and in to Soltaire before heading back to Walvis Bay.

 • Suggest places that you might stop for photographs.

 • Where would you fill up with petrol?

f) What other evidence is there on the map that suggests that this part of Namibia is well suited for adventure tourism?

ICT ACTIVITY

Few people know about Namibia and the potential that it offers for adventure tourism. You have been asked to produce a single-sided advert to appear in a national newspaper promoting Namibia as a centre for adventure tourism. Use the information in this section together with internet research to design an informative and attractive advert. Remember that you are focusing on adventure tourism.

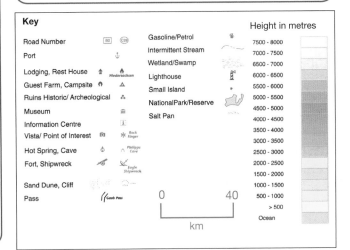

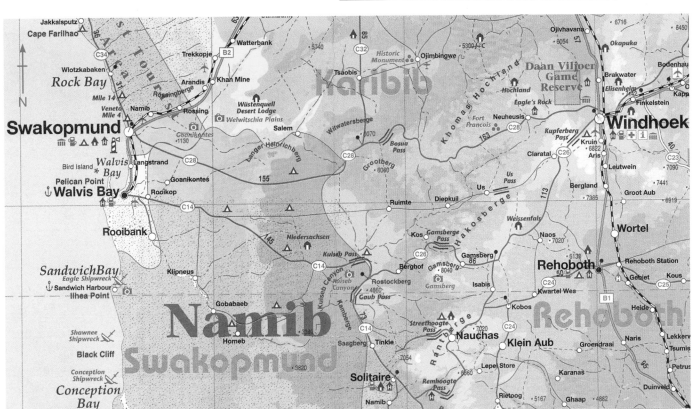

▲ **Figure 10   Namibia map extract**

D Tourism in paradise: the Maldives

One of the most popular destinations for wealthy Europeans is the Maldives, a small group of islands in the Indian Ocean (Figure 11). The first tourists arrived in the early 1970s, and since then tourism has grown rapidly to become the most important economic activity on the islands. There are now over 80 purpose-built resorts and about 600,000 people visit the Maldives every year.

The Maldives is marketed as an upmarket tourist destination catering for people with plenty of money! It offers luxury accommodation in purpose built resorts and aims to indulge and pamper its guests. Enjoying a warm tropical climate and surrounded by pristine blue seas (Figure 12), the Maldives caters for people keen to mix sunbathing and spa treatments with scuba diving, shark fishing and windsurfing.

Whilst tourism has brought wealth and employment to the islands, there are a number of important issues that need to be considered as tourism continues to expand.

- Future development must be done sensitively to minimise the impact on the natural environment and on ecosystems.

- The coral reef that surrounds the islands is one of the major attractions for tourists (see page 62). It is, however, extremely fragile and is easily damaged by boat anchors or even human touch.

- The luxury resorts (Figure 13) use a large amount of electricity and produce a lot of waste.

- If the islands continue to be developed they risk becoming overcrowded.

- Shark hunting has been an issue in the past and in some areas sharks have disappeared. They are hunted for their fins, which are a culinary delicacy.

- Workers in the tourism industry are often poorly paid.

- Global warming poses a real threat to the Maldives. The islands are very vulnerable to sea level rise.

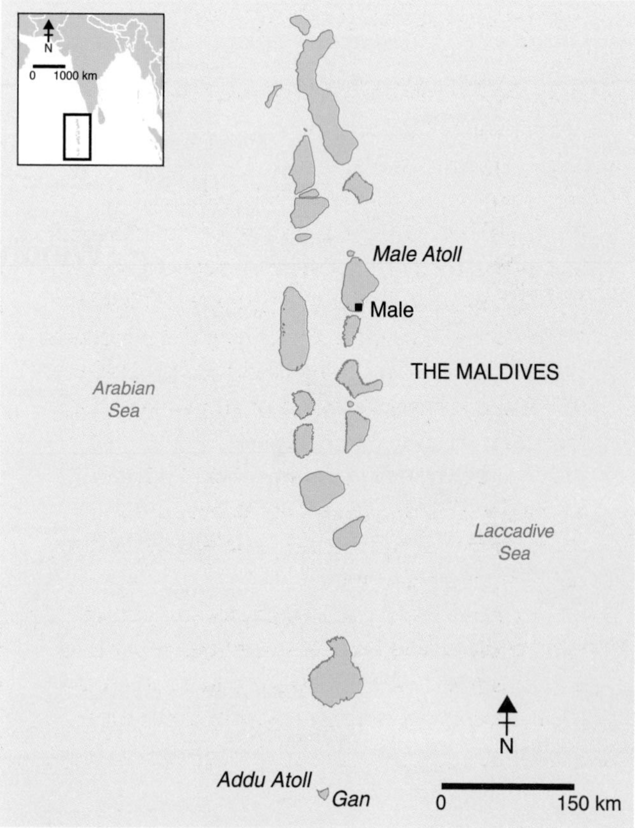

▲ **Figure 11   The Maldives**

▲ **Figure 12   The Maldives: a tropical paradise**

▲ **Figure 13   A tourist resort in the Maldives**

Activity

7 Study Figure 13. Before attempting this activity, **try to access** http://en.wikipedia.org/wiki/Tourism_in_the_Maldives **and read the section 'Overview of a tropical resort'.**

a) Draw a large sketch of the photograph to show the main features of the coast and the resort.

b) Add the following labels to your sketch.
   • resort
   • shallow tropical sea
   • pier and luxury boats
   • sandy beach

c) Now try to add a few more labels to describe other features you can see.

d) Notice towards the botom of the photo that there are several lengths of artificial breakwaters around the island. Why do you think they have been constructed?

e) Suggest further developments that could take place on the island.

f) What are the advantages and disadvantages of allowing further developments to take place on this island?

 ICT ACTIVITY

Access the Tourism in the Maldives website at www.tourisminmaldives.com.
• Click 'Tourism in Maldives'.
• Scroll to the bottom and click 'Weather in Maldives'. Describe the climate of the Maldives and suggest why this is an attraction to tourists.
• Now go back and click 'Geography of Maldives'. Write a few sentences describing the geography of the islands. How many islands are there? What are the islands made of and what are their main features?
• Now go back once again and click 'Culture of Maldives'. Describe some of the cultural characteristics of the local people, such as their religion, crafts and music.
• Having read about the geography and culture of the Maldives, write a few sentences describing why it is important to ensure that tourism is developed in a sustainable way in the future.

E Ecotourism: Rancho Margot, Costa Rica

In recent years, people have become concerned about the negative impacts of tourism on local communities and natural environments.

In response to these issues, a new form of tourism has developed called **ecotourism**. Ecotourism aims to educate small groups of tourists about the natural environment and introduce them to local cultures. Local communities benefit from ecotourism by acting as guides, by producing food and crafts, and in constructing and maintaining the accommodation. Ecotourism resorts strive to be sustainable. They make use of renewable energy, minimise waste and recycle. Buildings are constructed using local materials rather than imported bricks and concrete.

Rancho Margot Resort, Costa Rica

Costa Rica in Central America offers a huge range of attractive landscapes for tourists who are interested in the natural world, including towering volcanoes, sandy beaches and tropical rainforests (Figure 14). There are a large number of ecotourism projects in Costa Rica, including Rancho Margot.

Rancho Margot is ideally situated on the shores of Lake Arenal close to several natural attractions, including Arenal volcano, the Children's Eternal Rainforest and the Monteverde Biosphere Reserve.

The resort has been developed to be sustainable and self-sufficient. Water comes from local springs and much of the food is produced on site. There is an organic garden producing fruit and vegetables, and animals such as pigs and chickens are reared. Rancho Margot is self-sufficient in energy, producing electricity from a water-powered micro-turbine. A biodigester converts organic waste into methane gas that can be used for heating and cooking. Local materials are used in the construction of buildings, paths and bridges, and a small river has been dammed to create freshwater swimming pools (Figure 15).

Rancho Margot offers a variety of educational and relaxation courses and it provides a base for more adventurous activities such as horse riding, kayaking and trekking. Tourists can learn about medicinal plants, small-scale energy production and growing organic food.

▲ **Figure 14 Natural attractions in Costa Rica**

Activities

8 Study Figure 14.

a) The man who is pointing in the photograph is a guide from the local community. How do foreign tourists benefit from having a local guide?

b) Why is it a good thing for local people to be able to act as guides?

c) What do you think the guide is saying to the tourists?

d) Describe the natural landscape in the photo.

e) Why is it important to have only small groups visiting this area?

f) Why is this a good example of ecotourism?

9 Study Figure 15.

a) What local materials have been used to construct the swimming pools?

b) Is there any other evidence in the photo that local materials have been used in buildings at Rancho Margot?

c) There are many short trails providing access into the rainforest such as the one you can see in the photo. Why do you think these are popular with tourists?

d) If you were to take a photo from the same place in 25 years' time, would you expect to see any changes? Explain your answer.

e) From what you have learned about Rancho Margot would you like to stay there? Give reasons for your answer.

ICT ACTIVITY

Imagine that the Geography and Biology Departments at your school are planning to organise a trip to Costa Rica. They are keen to spend some time in an ecotourism resort to try to give pupils a genuine experience of the country and its people. Your teachers want your opinion of Rancho Margot.

Use the Rancho Margot website at www.ranchomargot.org to see if this would be a good place to stay. You need to consider the accommodation (can it cope with a group of about 20 people, relatively cheaply?) and the activities available (is there a good range of things to do?). What can you find out about the Children's Eternal Rainforest and Monteverde Biosphere Reserve? Is it possible to get close to Arenal volcano?

Produce an illustrated report (based on your research), saying whether you think your school should stay at Rancho Margot and why. Include a map (see website above) to show the location of Rancho Margot.

▲ **Figure 15   Freshwater swimming pools at Rancho Margot**

F Issue: Should tourists be allowed to visit Antarctica?

For millions of years, Antarctica has been cut off from the rest of the world due to its remoteness and its harsh climate. This has now begun to change. Antarctica is fast becoming one of the most popular 'extreme' tourist destinations (Figure 16).

Cruise liners are now capable of carrying up to 3,000 passengers to the shores of the continent, where many disembark for just a few hours to explore this unique environment (Figure 17). In 2008, an estimated 45,000 people visited Antarctica. This is likely to increase as global warming opens up new shipping passages.

What are the threats associated with tourism?

- **Danger** – Some of the large modern cruise liners are not built to cope with the extreme conditions.

- **Pollution** – Antarctica is a pristine environment that could quickly deteriorate if polluted by waste, oil spills, etc.

- **Invasive species** – The Antarctic ecosystem is very fragile and could easily be damaged by the introduction of alien species, such as plants and insects. Cruise ships can introduce new marine species into the area, for example, attached to their hulls (such as mussels).

What can be done to prevent damage to Antarctica?

The International Association of Antarctic Tour Operators promotes sustainable tourism. It has published guidelines to limit the number of tourists allowed onshore.

▲ **Figure 17 Tourism in Antarctica**

Activity

10 The aim of this activity is for you to decide whether tourists should be banned from Antarctica. If not, then should their numbers be severely restricted? How could this be done fairly? You may like to debate this issue as a class after you have completed your individual research.

Consider the arguments *in favour* and *against* tourism in Antarctica by looking at the following websites. Make some notes as you go along and use them to back up your own point of view when you have made up your mind. Use some photographs to support your arguments.

Times Online article at www.timesonline.co.uk/toltravel/holiday_type/cruises/article1886800.ece

International Association of Antarctic Tour Operators at www.iaato.org/tourism_overview.html

British Antarctic Survey at www.antarctica.ac.uk/about_antarctica/tourism/index.php

BBC article published in 2009 at http://news.bbc.co.uk/1/hi/sci/tech/8005467.stm

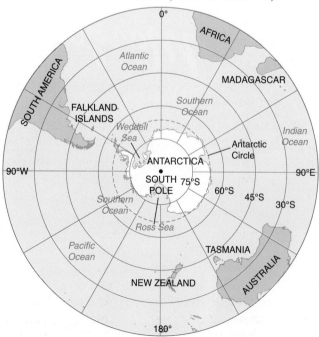

▲ **Figure 16 Location map of Antarctica**

Global Environmental Issues

10

A Global environmental issues

In this chapter, we are going to study some global environmental issues. While we are doing this, we will link together some of the topics we have covered in this book.

The natural environment, the vegetation, soils and living organisms are largely determined by climatic factors. People interact with the natural environment by exploiting its resources through farming, mining and fishing. We cut down trees, add chemicals to the soil and construct towns and cities. The natural environment affects us and, increasingly, we affect it (Figure 1).

Sustainable development is about improving the quality of people's lives without damaging the environment. It is perfectly possible to use the Earth's resources in a controlled manner, to avoid damaging the environment on which we all depend. Environmental issues often arise when our relationship with the environment is not in balance (Figure 2, page 124).

▲ **Figure 1   The balance between people and the environment**

Activities

1 For this activity you should work in pairs to discuss the following questions. Study Figure 1.

  a) Do you think people are living in balance with the environment in this photo? Give reasons for your answer.

  b) If you were to go to the area shown in the photo, what would you investigate at first hand, to see if your answer to (a) was correct?

  c) Suggest some changes that might take place in the next ten years that could affect the balance between the people and the natural environment. Describe the possible impacts of these changes.

  d) Should we be concerned about the future of the environment?

2 Study Figure 2 (page 124).

  a) Which of the environmental issues in Figure 2 concerns you most? Justify your selection.

  b) Can you think of any environmental issues that are not represented in Figure 2?

  c) Some people say that the biggest environmental issue on the planet is the rapid growth of the world's population. Do you agree?

  d) With the help of the internet, create your own version of Figure 2. Try to include some recent issues that have arisen this year. Media websites (such as the BBC) will provide you with some examples. Give your work a title, print it and display in your classroom.

Major oil spill in South Korea, 2007. A barge collided with a crude oil carrier, spilling 2.8 million gallons of crude oil. Thirty beaches were affected, half the region's sea farms lost their fish stocks and sea gulls, mallard ducks and other sea life were found tarred by the oil.

Waste in the Pacific, February 2008, hit the headlines in being described as a 'plastic soup'.

Waste is accumulating in landfill sites in China.

Pacific Ocean

Oil spills and poor land management in the Niger Delta of Nigeria has caused 5 to 10 per cent of mangrove forests to disappear.

Soil erosion is a problem. Some of it goes into the rivers. The rivers, choked with soil, move towards the sea.

The boom in palm oil production and plantations in Borneo has affected the jungles and is endangering the orang-utan population. An assessment by the UN in 2007 found that the apes will be virtually eliminated in the wild within two decades if current deforestation trends continue.

Coral bleaching on the Great Barrier Reef is due to an increase in water temperatures. This damages and destroys the coral reefs, and the sea life that depends on them.

▲ **Figure 2 Recent global environmental issues**

B Spreading deserts and soil erosion

According to the United Nations, tens of millions of people could be forced from their homes as a result of the spread of the world's deserts. This process is called **desertification**. Within the next ten years, some 50 million people could be displaced. A report published by the United Nations in 2007, described desertification as 'the greatest environmental challenge of our times'.

Look at Figure 3. Notice that desertification is occurring throughout the world. See how it is most severe around the edges of the world's deserts.

Once land has turned into desert, the soil becomes dry and dusty. It is easily blown or washed away by strong winds and the occasional torrential rainstorm. This removal of soil is called **soil erosion**. Soils take thousands of years to form but can be washed away in just a matter of days.

▲ **Figure 4   Desertification on the edge of the Gobi desert**

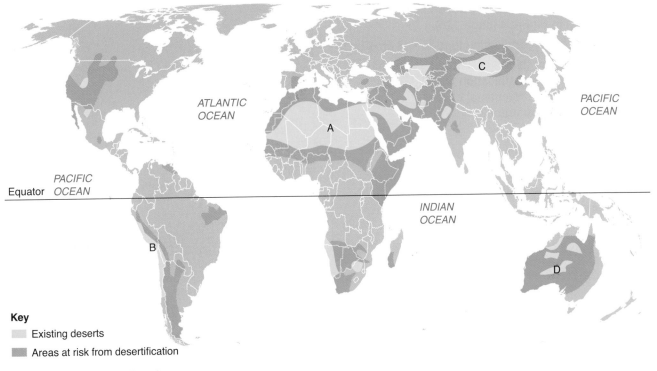

Key

Existing deserts

Areas at risk from desertification

▲ **Figure 3   Desertification**

Desertification in the Sahel

Look back at Figure 3 on page 125 and notice that many parts of Africa suffer from desertification. One area is the Sahel, which forms a broad belt to the south of the Sahara Desert. Here climatic conditions are particularly extreme, with very high summer temperatures and unreliable rainfall. The vegetation is mostly poor quality grass, with some low shrubs and bushes.

Despite the harsh conditions, traditional tribes have learned to cope with the lack of rainfall and the intense summer heat. They use the sparse vegetation as grazing for their animals and live a nomadic life moving with their herds from place to place in search of fresh pastures. This type of agriculture is called **nomadic pastoralism** (Figure 5). The people of the Sahel are living on the very edge of survival and their lands are being increasingly threatened by desertification.

Causes of desertification in the Sahel

There are several causes of desertification in the Sahel. These include natural factors such as unreliable rainfall (possibly connected to climate change), and human factors such as **overgrazing**, where too many animals are grazed on an area of land. Overgrazing can result from an increase in population or from restrictions in the amount of land available for grazing. Other causes of desertification can include the removal of vegetation for firewood, and over-pumping of groundwater for irrigation, which can lead to a fall in the water table causing plants to die. In almost all cases, however, desertification is the result of a complex interaction of natural and human factors. The people who suffer the most are often the poorest, in this case the nomadic pastoralists.

Activities

3 Study Figures 3 and 4 (page 125).

  a) What is meant by the term 'desertification'?

  b) Use the atlas map on pages 134–35 to identify the names of the deserts A–D that have serious problems of desertification at their margins.

  c) Describe the effects of desertification shown in Figure 4 (page 125).

  d) How can desertification lead to soil erosion?

  e) Why do you think the United Nations has described desertification as being the 'greatest environmental challenge of our time'? Do you agree?

4 Study Figure 5.

  a) What animals are being herded in the photograph?

  b) Describe the landscape in the photograph.

  c) What is the evidence that this is a harsh environment in which to live?

  d) How might nomadic pastoralists like the person in the photograph be part of the problem of desertification?

  e) How might the people also be part of the solution to the problem?

▲ **Figure 5   Nomadic pastoralism in the Sahel region of Africa**

Solutions to desertification

Reducing the rate of desertification and attempting to reverse the process is a massive challenge.

In the Sahel, water harvesting is encouraged by the construction of lines of small stone dams (Figure 6). Local people do this by placing large rocks along the contours of the land and infilling using smaller stones. In this way, the low stone dams help to trap soil and water flowing downhill following periods of heavy rain. The dams lead to a build-up of soil for farming and help to prevent soil erosion.

Other projects include the creation of demonstration farms to educate local people in new sustainable farming techniques and to demonstrate new types of drought-resistant crops. Sustainable forms of cooking such as **solar ovens** (Figure 7) are being introduced as alternatives to using firewood.

Activity

5 Study Figure 6. Imagine that you are a project officer working for a charity in the Sahel. You have been asked to design a set of instructions for a group of enthusiastic volunteers who are going to help a local community construct water-harvesting dams. Contours have already been marked on the bare stony ground by a group of experts.

Your instructions, to be written on a single side of paper, need to include the following details:

- You need to give the volunteers brief background information about the water-harvesting scheme. They need to be able to talk to the local people about what the scheme involves. They need to convince the community of the benefits of this project.

- The volunteers need to know what to do. Ideally, use simple sketches to show clearly how to construct the small stone dams.

▲ **Figure 6 Water harvesting in the Sahel**

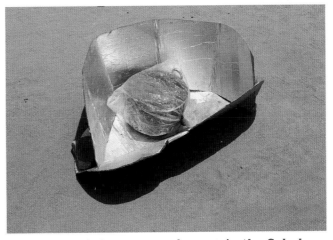

▲ **Figure 7 Solar-powered ovens in the Sahel**

 ICT ACTIVITY

Your school has decided to have a non-uniform day in aid of a charity working in Africa. The charity co-ordinator at your school has invited ideas from pupils. You have decided to make a case for solar-powered ovens to reduce the need for people to collect firewood in areas threatened by desertification.

Use the internet to find out more about solar-powered ovens. How do they work? What are their benefits? How much do they cost? Is there a charity organisation that supplies them (see the Solar Cookers International website below)? Having done your research, you need to write a short paper to try to convince your school's charity co-ordinator that this is a good cause for which to raise money. You will need to be convincing!

Websites:

http://en.wikipedia.org/wiki/Solar_ovens
http://solar.envirohub.net/solar-ovens-and-cookers.htm
http://solarcookers.org

C Tropical rainforests, chicken nuggets and orang-utans

Many people are concerned about the rate of **deforestation** (Figure 8). Each year an area of forest almost twice the size of Denmark is lost. At the current rate of deforestation, the entire world's tropical rainforests could completely disappear within 100 years.

Tropical rainforests are unique ecosystems that support an incredible variety of wildlife. In being described as the 'lungs of the world', they play a vital part in absorbing carbon dioxide and emitting oxygen.

▲ **Figure 9   Oil palm in Malaysia**

▲ **Figure 8   Deforestation**

Activity

6 Study Figure 8.

a) How is the rainforest being cleared?

b) Describe the likely impact of the rainforest clearance on the following:
   - wildlife in the forest
   - local tribal communities who live in the forest
   - the atmosphere.

c) Why do you think the rainforest has been cleared from here?

Why is land being deforested?

Most deforestation is to clear land for farming. Small-scale 'slash and burn' creates land for local communities to provide food for themselves. This may be sustainable as long as the forest is given enough time to recover before being cleared again.

Large-scale forest clearance for commercial farming is much more destructive. This creates land for cattle ranching or growing commercial crops such as soya and oil palm (Figure 9). Soybean grown in Brazil is used to feed chickens in England that are then processed into fast-food chicken nuggets!

The clearance of rainforests by burning pumps huge quantities of greenhouse gases (such as carbon dioxide) into the atmosphere, increasing global warming. It damages natural ecosystems, leading to some species becoming endangered or even extinct. Land is laid to waste and becomes prone to soil erosion. In so many ways, deforestation is harmful to the environment.

How can deforestation be controlled?

Understandably, many countries wish to exploit their tropical rainforests in order to create wealth and improve the quality of people's lives. Local rainforest communities may themselves depend on deforestation as a source of income. Therefore, is it unreasonable for the richer countries of the world to expect these countries not to develop their own resources? Imagine the UK being put under pressure by foreign countries to stop extracting oil and gas from the North Sea!

Whilst deforestation continues to be an important global issue, many countries have begun to address the problem.

● **Sustainable management:** Some countries, for example Malaysia, have introduced a sustainable management programme. Trees are selectively felled and new trees planted (Figure 11). Despite these good intentions, illegal logging still remains an issue in remote regions, such as Borneo where wildlife such as orang-utans are under threat (Figure 11).

● **Carbon payments:** In Sierra Leone in West Africa, a 75,000 hectare forest park called Gola Forest has been established (Figure 12). Aid agencies, France and the European Commission have set up a £6 million fund to pay for the park's running costs and provide local people with an income. In return, the forest will be protected and used instead for tourism and scientific research. Payments such as these are called carbon payments because they reduce potential carbon emissions (no burning) as well as absorbing carbon dioxide from the air.

▲ **Figure 10   Orang-utan in Borneo**

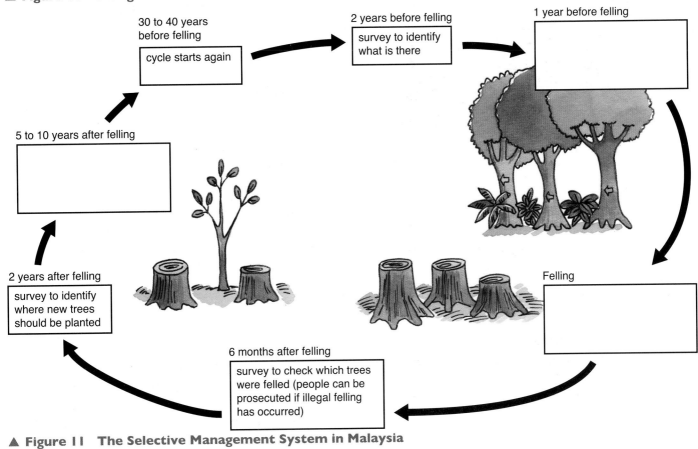

30 to 40 years before felling

cycle starts again

2 years before felling

survey to identify what is there

1 year before felling

5 to 10 years after felling

2 years after felling

survey to identify where new trees should be planted

6 months after felling

survey to check which trees were felled (people can be prosecuted if illegal felling has occurred)

Felling

▲ **Figure 11   The Selective Management System in Malaysia**

● **Consumer power:** In a similar way that Fairtrade has created consumer demand for certain food products, forest certificates such as the Forest Stewardship Council certificate (Figure 12) are doing much the same for timber. If a forest has been well managed, its trees qualify for a certificate and, increasingly, consumers are only choosing to buy certificated trees and paper.

Whilst the international community generally agree that rainforests need to be protected, deforestation seems likely to be a serious environmental issue in the future.

▲ **Figure 12 Forestry Stewardship Council icon**

Activities

7 Study Figure 14. For this activity you will need a blank world outline.

  a) Use a series of proportional bars or circles to represent the information in Figure 15 on your world map. To do this, you need to work out an appropriate scale for your bars. Keep the horizontal width of each bar the same.

  b) Use your scale to draw each bar. Try to locate the base of the bar as close to the appropriate country as you can. Try to avoid overlapping the bars.

  c) Use a single colour to shade the bars.

  d) Give your map a title.

  e) Brazil loses the largest area of rainforest annually. Why do you think it is not in the top ten?

8 Study Figure 11 (page 129).

  a) Make a large copy of the selective management system diagram.

  b) Complete the diagram by writing the following labels in their correct places.

    • Trees to be felled are tagged and the direction of felling is painted on the trunks

    • Felling is carried out under the guidance of state foresters

    • Unwanted climbers are removed and new trees planted

  c) Why is it important that experts identify the trees to be felled and the direction of felling?

  d) State foresters keep detailed records both before and after felling. Why is this important?

  e) Why do you think it is important to leave the trees for up to 40 years before they are cut down again?

  f) Do you think this system is a sustainable form of management? Explain your answer.

◀ **Figure 13 Gola Forest park, Sierra Leone**

▶ **Figure 14 Top ten worst rates of primary tropical deforestation (2000–2005)**
NB Primary rainforest is rainforest that shows no signs of past or present human activity. It is the most diverse ecosystem on the planet.

1	Nigeria	55.7%
2	Vietnam	54.5%
3	Cambodia	29.4%
4	Sri Lanka	15.2%
5	Malawi	14.9%
6	Indonesia	12.9%
7	North Korea	9.3%
8	Nepal	9.1%
9	Panama	6.7%
10	Guatemala	6.4%

D Plastic soup in the Pacific Ocean

In 1997, an American oceanographer called Charles Moore made a shocking discovery (Figure 15). He discovered a vast plastic garbage patch floating in the Pacific Ocean. In 2008, scientists reported that this mass of floating flotsam had increased rapidly and now covered an area equivalent to twice the size of the USA (Figure 16).

Stretching from California across the northern Pacific, almost to Japan, this vast plastic 'soup' is concentrated into two distinct patches (Figure 17, page 132). Amongst the rubbish is everything from footballs and kayaks, to Lego blocks and carrier bags. As Figure 17 shows it is caught up in a complex circulation system driven by large-scale underwater ocean currents. The water currents keep the waste afloat and prevent it from sinking to the ocean floor.

The plastic waste in the Pacific is thought to be responsible for the death of millions of seabirds every year, as well as more than 100,000 marine mammals. Dutch scientists recently carried out a study of seabirds. They found that the stomach of one bird (that died in Belgium) contained 1,603 separate pieces of plastic. The stomach of an Albatross (found on a remote Pacific Island) contained a cigarette lighter, a toothbrush, a toy robot and a tampon applicator (Figure 18, page 132). All these items came from waste floating on the sea and dumped by people from boats, oil platforms or from land.

▲ **Figure 15   Captain Charles Moore floating in the Pacific plastic soup**

▲ **Figure 16   Waste washed up on the shore of Kamilo Beach, Hawaii**

Activities

9 Study Figures 15, 16 and 17 (pages 131–132).

a) Make a list of the items of waste shown in the photographs.

b) What do you think the people are doing in Figure 16?

c) Amongst the waste is a dead shark. You suspect that its death may be related to the pollution in the sea. What evidence would you look for to support your suspicions?

d) Much of the waste in Figure 16 is from land sources. Use Figure 17 to suggest where it may have come from.

e) Apart from land sources, suggest two other possible sources of the waste.

f) What is meant by the saying 'out of sight, out of mind' and how does it apply to the issue of marine pollution?

10 Study Figure 17.

a) Describe the location of the Eastern Garbage Patch.

b) Suggest which countries the Eastern Garbage Patch might affect.

c) Refer to the cross section in Figure 17. Describe the location of the layer of garbage.

d) The garbage in the Pacific has only recently been discovered. Can you suggest why?

11 Study Figure 18. Imagine that you work for an environmental group concerned with marine pollution. The director wants you to write a brief press report based on the photograph. It must be no longer than 100 words.

▲ **Figure 18   The stomach contents of a dead albatross found in Hawaii**

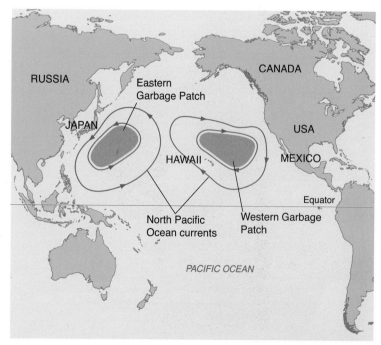

▲ **Figure 17   The vast circulating Pacific garbage tip**

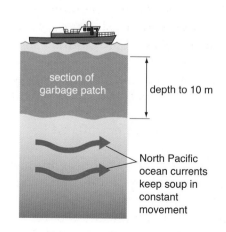

E Issue: Can geographers save the world?

Geography is the key to understanding places and people. It helps us to understand the interactions between the human and physical processes that shape our world. Geographers are uniquely placed to consider the 'big picture' when it comes to managing the world in which we live. We are passionate about looking after the planet, and making sure that future generations will be able to benefit from the resources it has to offer. The concept of sustainability is rooted in geography and it has been a consistent theme throughout this series.

Look at Figure 19. In studying geography you learn a wide range of really important skills. These include the ability to carry out meaningful investigations that are accurate and reliable. Geographers develop a multiple range of presentational skills. Consider all the skills you have developed recently, such as writing reports, observing maps and photos, working in small groups, engaging in discussions or forming your own opinion. These are skills that are highly valued in most jobs. Consider, too, how you have developed your ICT skills by using the internet for research and by using programs (such as PowerPoint®) to make presentations. You will continue to develop all these important skills, as well as broadening your global knowledge and understanding, as you move on to study GCSE Geography.

With our broad knowledge and understanding of the world, and our highly developed flexible skills, geographers are indeed well placed to help save the world!

Activities

12 Study Figure 19.

a) Make a list of the items that the girl is carrying.

b) Each item represents a particular skill that she has developed as a geographer. Can you suggest what these skills are?

c) What other skills will she have developed as a geographer, that are not shown in Figure 19?

13 The Royal Geographical Society wants your help! It wants to promote the subject and encourage even more people to study GCSE Geography. It has decided to produce a series of posters promoting the study of geography, by showing how it is relevant in today's world. The posters are to be designed by Year 9 pupils so that they will appeal directly to the same age group.

a) Flick back through this book, to remind yourself of the kind of things that you have studied and the skills that you have developed. Make a rough list of the aspects that you think could be included on a poster.

b) Design your poster, making use of carefully chosen images from the internet. Don't forget to include a catchy title. There is no need to include details about GCSE. You are just concerned with promoting the subject itself as being important and interesting to study.

▲ **Figure 19 Geography: education for life**

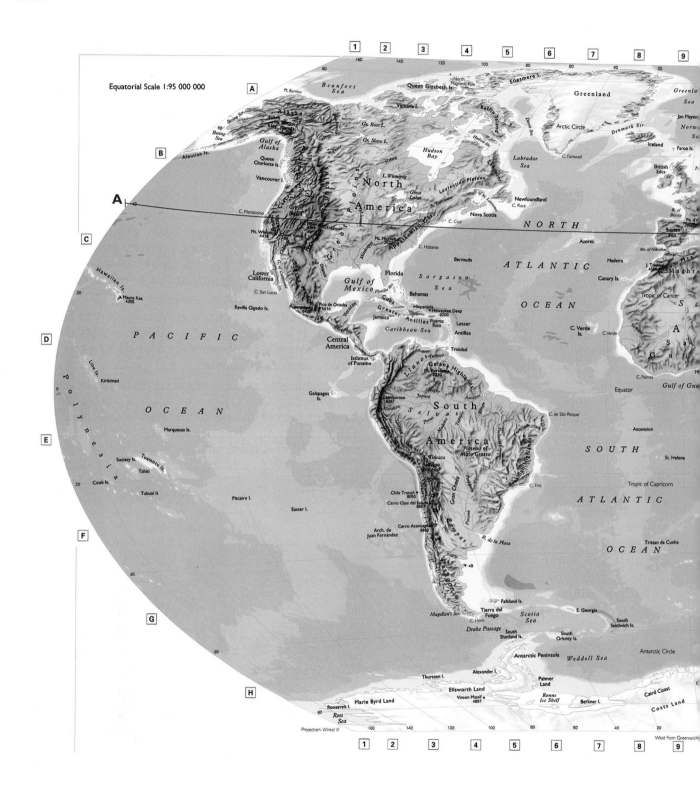

Equatorial Scale 1:95 000 000

Projection: Winkel III

West from Greenwich

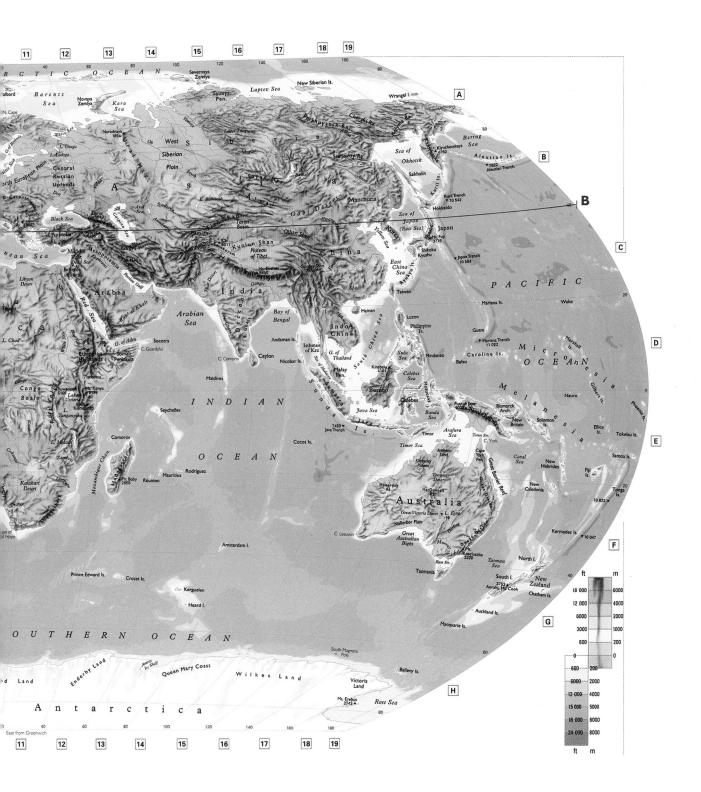

A R C T I C   O C E A N

Barents
Sea

N. Cape

Novaya
Zemlya

Kara
Sea

Severnaya
Zemlya

Taimyr
Pen.

Laptev Sea

New Siberian Is.

Wrangel I.

A

Svalbard

Gulf of Bothnia

White Sea

L. Onega

L. Ladoga

Narodnaya
1894

Yenisey

Ob

West
Siberian
Plain

Irtysh

S   i   b   e   r   i   a

Lower Tunguska

Stanovoy Ra.

Verkhoyansk Ra.

Chersky Ra.

Kolyma

Kamchatka

Klyuchevskaya
4750

Dezhneva

Bering
Sea

Aleutian Is.

7822
Aleutian Trench

B

North European Plain

Central
Russian
Uplands

Don

Dnieper

Volga

Caspian Sea

Ural Mts.

Syr Darya

L. Balkhash

Altai

Sayan Ra.

Baikal

Gobi Desert

Manchuria

Sea of
Okhotsk

Sakhalin

Kuril Is.

Kuril Trench
10 542

Hokkaido

B

Black Sea

Anatolia

Elbrus
5642

Caucasus

Aral
Sea

Amu Darya

-28

Tien Shan

Tarim
Basin

Tarim

Qilian Shan

Hwang Ho

Yellow
Sea

Korea
(East Sea)

Sea of
Japan

Japan

Mt. Fuji
3776

C

nean
Sea

Middle
East

Dead Sea
Isthmus
of Suez

Euphrates

Tigris

Elburz
5604

Persian Gulf

K2
8611

Kunlun Shan

Plateau
of Tibet

Mt. Everest
8850

Tsang Po

Tsin Ling

Gobi Desert

China

Shikoku

Kyushu

Japan Trench
10 554

C

Libyan
Desert

a

Arabia

Red Sea

Rub' al Khali

Gulf of Aden

Socotra

C. Guardafui

Indus

Thar Desert

Ganges

India

Western Ghats

Eastern Ghats

Brahmaputra

Irrawaddy

Salween

Mekong

Bay of
Bengal

Indo
China

Hainan

East
China
Sea

Taiwan

Ryukyu Is.

P A C I F I C

Mariana Is.

Wake

20

D

Tibesti

Nile

Blue Nile

White Nile

L. Chad

Ethiopian
Highlands

-155

Somali
Peninsula

Arabian
Sea

Maldives

Andaman Is.

Nicobar Is.

Ceylon

Isthmus
of Kra

G. of
Thailand

Malay
Pen.

Str. of Malacca

South China
Sea

Sulu
Sea

Mindanao

Luzon

Philippine
Is.

Guam

Belau

Caroline Is.

Mariana Trench
11 022

Micronesia

Marshall
Is.

Gilbert Is.

Nauru

Phoenix Is.

D

Congo
Basin

Ruwenzori
5109

Mt. Kenya
5199

Kilimanjaro

L. Victoria

L. Turkana

Seychelles

I N D I A N

Cocos Is.

Java Trench
7450

Sunda Is.

Borneo

Kinabalu
4101

Celebes
Sea

Celebes

Java Sea

Moluccas

Banda
Sea

Puncak Jaya
5029

New Guinea

Bismarck
Arch.

New
Britain

Solomon
Is.

M e l a n e s i a

Ellice
Is.

Tokelau Is.

O C E A N

E

Okavango

L. Mweru

L. Tanganyika

L. Malawi

Zambezi

Comoros

Madagascar

Mozambique Chan.

Pic Boby
2658

Réunion

Mauritius

Rodriguez

O C E A N

Cocos Is.

Timor

Timor Sea

Arafura
Sea

Torres Str.

C. York

Arnhem
Land

Cape
York
Park

Coral
Sea

New
Hebrides

New
Caledonia

Fiji
Is.

Samoa Is.

Tonga
10 822

20

E

Kalahari
Desert

Orange

Limpopo

Prince Edward Is.

Crozet Is.

Kerguelen

Heard I.

Amsterdam I.

C. Leeuwin

Hamersley
Ra.

Great Victoria Desert

Nullarbor Plain

Tanami
Desert

Katherine
Plateau

MacDonnell

L. Eyre
-16

Great
Australian
Bight

A u s t r a l i a

Murray

Darling

Kosciuszko
2230

Bass Str.

Tasman
Sea

North I.

South I.

Aoraki Mt Cook
3753

New
Zealand

Chatham Is.

Kermadec Is.
10 047

F

pe of
d Hope

Tasmania

ft   m

18 000   6000
12 000   4000
6000   2000
3000   1000
600   200
0   0
600   200
6000   2000
12 000   4000
15 000   5000
18 000   6000
24 000   8000

ft   m

40

20

0

20

40

S O U T H E R N   O C E A N

Amery Ice Shelf

South Magnetic
Pole

G

d Land

Enderby Land

Queen Mary Coast

Wilkes Land

Victoria
Land

Balleny Is.

H

A n t a r c t i c a

Mt. Erebus
3743

Ross
Sea

60

80

Human Geography of the World

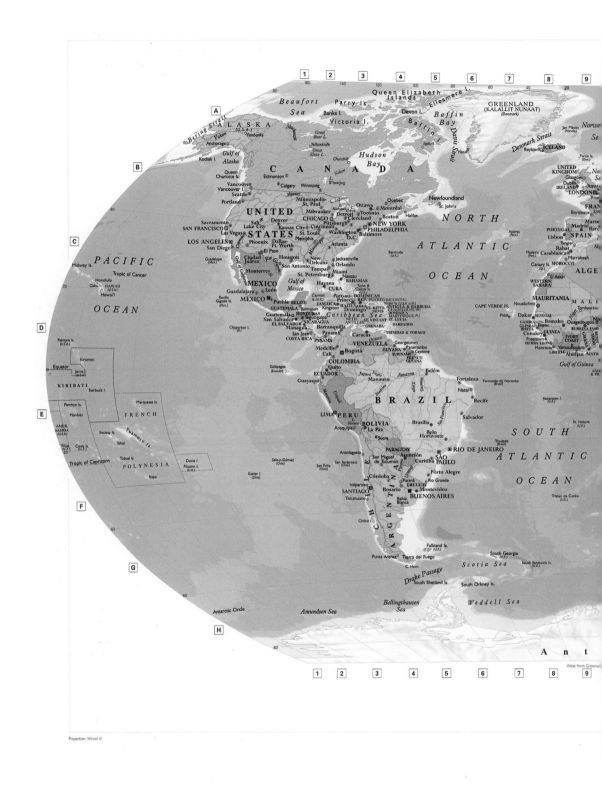

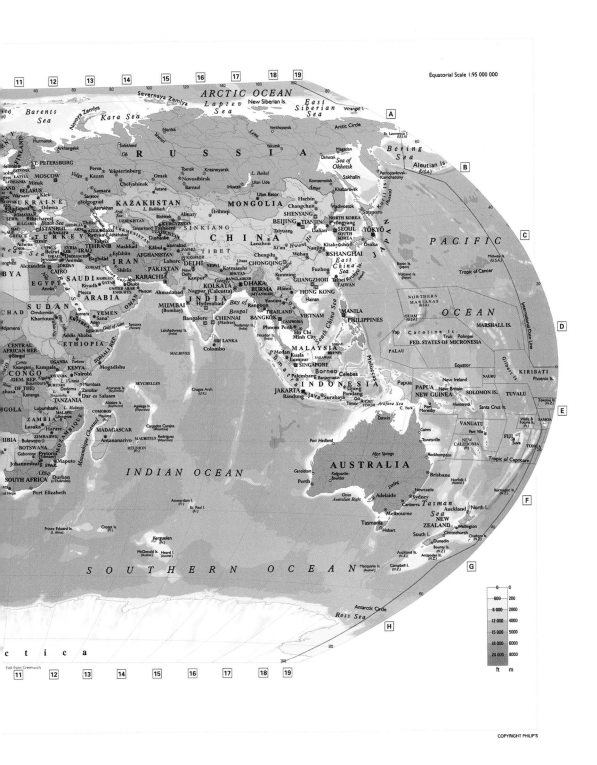

Equatorial Scale 1:95 000 000

ARCTIC OCEAN

Severnaya Zemlya
Laptev
Sea
New Siberian Is.
East
Siberian
Sea
Wrangel I.

A

Barents
Sea
Novaya Zemlya
Kara Sea
Arctic Circle
St. Lawrence I.
(U.S.A.)

Murmansk
Norilsk
Verkhoyansk
Bering
Sea
B

FINLAND
Arkhangelsk
Solekhard
Ob
Yenisey
Yakutsk
Magadan
Okhotsk
Petropavlovsk-
Kamchatskiy
Aleutian Is.
(U.S.A.)

ST. PETERSBURG
R U S S I A
Sea of
Okhotsk
Sakhalin

stholm
ESTONIA
MOSCOW
Volga
Perm
Yekaterinburg
Tomsk
Krasnoyarsk
L. Baikal
Komsomolsk

gen LATVIA
Kazan
Khabarovsk

AND
LITHUANIA
Minsk
Samara
Chelyabinsk
Omsk
Novosibirsk
Irkutsk
Amur
Vladivostok

que
BELARUS
Volgograd
Saratov
Astana
Barnaul
Ulan Ude
Harbin
Sapporo

Warsaw
KAZAKHSTAN
Bishkek
Almaty
Ürümqi
MONGOLIA
Changchun
SHENYANG
NORTH KOREA
Pyŏngyang
TŌKYŌ

UKRAINE
Aral
Sea
KYRGYZSTAN
Ulan Bator
BEIJING
TIANJIN
SEOUL
SOUTH
KOREA

Kiev
Odessa
GEORGIA
Tashkent
SINKIANG
C H I N A
Taiyuan
Dalian
Osaka
J A P A N

Bucharest
UZBEKISTAN
Baku
TAJIKISTAN
Lanzhou
Xi'an
Hwang
Nanjing
Kitakyūshū

Black Sea
ARM.
Dushanbe
TIBET
Chengdu
Wuhan
SHANGHAI
East
China
Sea

ISTANBUL
Ankara
AZER.
TURKMENISTAN
Kābul
Islamabad
KASHMIR
CHONGQING
Fuzhou
Taipei

TURKEY
Tabriz
Ashkhabad
Mashhad
AFGHANISTAN
Lahore
JAMMU
Lhasa
Yangtze
TAIWAN

CYPRUS SYRIA
TEHRAN
Kunming
GUANGZHOU
HONG KONG

Damascus
Baghdad
I R A N
Eşfahān
PAKISTAN
DELHI
NEPAL
BHUTAN
Katmandu
Hainan

Beirut
Amman
IRAQ
Delhi
Kanpur
Ganges
BANGLADESH
DHAKA
BURMA
Hanoi

EGYPT
JORDAN
KUWAIT
Shīrāz
KARACHI
Ahmadābād
Nagpur
KOLKATA
(Calcutta)
(MYANMAR)

CAIRO
SAUDI
BAHRAIN
UNITED ARAB
EMIRATES
MUMBAI
(Bombay)
I N D I A
Hyderabad
Bay of
Bengal
Rangoon
Vientiane
VIETNAM

Mecca
ARABIA
QATAR
Muscat
OMAN
Bangalore
CHENNAI
(Madras)
THAILAND
BANGKOK
MANILA

SUDAN
YEMEN
Aden
Lakshadweep (India)
Andaman Is.
(India)
CAMBODIA
Phnom Penh
PHILIPPINES

Omdurmān
Sana'
Gulf of Aden
SRI LANKA
Nicobar Is.
(India)
Ho Chi
Minh City

Khartoum
DJIBOUTI
MALDIVES
Colombo
MALAYSIA
SABAH
BRUNEI

CENTRAL
AFRICAN REP.
ETHIOPIA
SOMALI REP.
Medan
Kuala
Lumpur
SARAWAK
SINGAPORE

UGANDA
KENYA
Mogadishu
Palembang
Borneo
Celebes
Banjarmasin

CONGO
(DEM. REP.
OF THE)
Nairobi
Chagos Arch.
(U.K.)
JAKARTA
I N D O N E S I A
Ujung
Pandang

TANZANIA
Dar es Salaam
SEYCHELLES
Bandung
Java
Surabaya

Lubumbashi
COMOROS
MADAGASCAR
INDIAN OCEAN
AUSTRALIA

ZAMBIA
Harare
MAURITIUS
Alice Springs
Brisbane

BOTSWANA
Antananarivo
Perth
Geraldton
Kalgoorlie-
Boulder

Johannesburg
Pretoria
Maputo
SWAZ.
SOUTH AFRICA
Durban
Adelaide
Sydney

P A C I F I C

O C E A N
Tropic of Cancer

NORTHERN
MARIANAS
(U.S.A.)

GUAM
(U.S.A.)
MARSHALL IS.
D

Caroline Is.
Yap
Truk
Pohnpei

PALAU
FED. STATES OF MICRONESIA

Equator
Gilbert Is.
KIRIBATI

NAURU
Phoenix Is.

New Ireland
New Britain
SOLOMON IS.
TUVALU
Tokelau Is.
(N.Z.)
E

Papua
PAPUA
NEW GUINEA
Santa Cruz Is.
Wallis &
Futuna Is.
(Fr.)
SAMOA

C. York
Port
Moresby
Honiara
VANUATU
Port Vila
FIJI
Suva
TONGA

Darwin
NEW
CALEDONIA
(Fr.)
Tropic of Capricorn

Cairns
Townsville
Rockhampton

Newcastle
Norfolk I.
(Austral.)
Kermadec Is.
(N.Z.)
F

Canberra
Melbourne
Tasman
Sea
Auckland
North I.
NEW
ZEALAND

Tasmania
Wellington
Chatham Is.
(N.Z.)

Hobart
South I.
Dunedin

Bonin Is.
(Japan)
Midway Is.
(U.S.A.)
C

Volcano Is.
(Japan)

International Date Line

Port Hedland

EGYPT
LIBYA
CHAD

Aswān
Red Sea
ERITREA
Asmera
DJIBOUTI
Addis Ababa

CONGO
Kisangani
Kampala
Kigali
RWANDA
L. Victoria
Mombasa

Bangui
Kanaga
BURUNDI
Bujumbura
Dodoma
Amirante Is.
(Seychelles)
L. Tanganyika
L. Malawi
Aldabra Is.
(Seychelles)

NGOLA
Kananga
MALAWI
Lilongwe
Mayotte
(Fr.)

Lusaka
ZIMBABWE
Bulawayo
MOZAMBIQUE
Cargados Carajos
(Mauritius)

IIBIA
Gaborone
LES.
Maseru
Cargados Carajos
Rodriguez
(Mauritius)

SOUTH AFRICA
(Tshwane)
RÉUNION
(Fr.)

Cape of
Good Hope
Port Elizabeth

Prince Edward Is.
(S. Africa)
Crozet Is.
(Fr.)
Amsterdam I.
(Fr.)
St. Paul I.
(Fr.)
Great
Australian Bight

Kerguelen
(Fr.)
McDonald Is.
(Austral.)
Heard I.
(Austral.)
Macquarie Is.
(N.Z.)
Campbell I.
(N.Z.)
Auckland Is.
(N.Z.)
Bounty Is.
(N.Z.)
Antipodes Is.
(N.Z.)

S O U T H E R N   O C E A N
G

Antarctic Circle
Ross Sea
H

c t i c a

East from Greenwich

0
500
5 000
12 000
15 000
18 000
24 000
ft

0
200
2000
4000
6000
8000
m

COPYRIGHT PHILIP'S

GLOSSARY

Adventure tourism   A form of tourism involving physical activities such as mountaineering, exploring and caving

Aggregate   Broken fragments of rock used, for example, in road building

Altitude   Height of the land above sea level

Aquifers   Underground reservoir of water held within porous rocks such as chalk

Aridity   Dryness resulting from the lack of rainfall. Deserts are arid environments

Birth rate   The number of live births per 1000 population in a year

Bush toilets   Open-air place used as a toilet

Bustees   Low income squatter housing in India

Canopy   The 'umbrella' formed by branches and leaves of a tree

Carbon payments   Payments made to offset carbon used in travel. Usually made to fund tree planting and similar projects aimed at carbon capture

Cereal crop   An arable crop such as wheat and barley. Rice – a type of grass – is also a cereal crop

Clearfelling   The wide scale destruction of forest involving the total clearance of huge areas rather than individual trees

Commercial   This is an operation (farming or industrial) that aims to create a profit by selling what is produced

Conservative (transform) margin   Where two tectonic plates are moving alongside each other, e.g. the San Andreas Fault in California, USA

Constructive margin   Where two tectonic plates are moving away from each other. Magma escapes to the surface to construct new plate

Consumer power   The power of the buyer. This can be important in shopping, for example where people wish to buy organically produced food

Continental shelf   Gently sloping sea floor on the edges of coastal regions

Continental slope   Steeper sloping sea floor between the continental shelf and the bottom of the oceans

Continentality   The effect on the weather and climate of being in the middle of a large land mass or being affected by conditions of this region. Usually dry with hot summers and cold winters

Convection currents   Currents of heat deep within the Earth that are responsible for tectonic plate movement

Death rate   The number of deaths per 1000 population in a year

Deforestation   The chopping down of trees

Delta   Low-lying land at the mouth of a river formed by deposition of silt as a river joins the sea or a lake. An example is the Nile delta

Desertification   The gradual creation of desert conditions often caused by overgrazing in semi-desert regions

Destructive margin   A tectonic plate margin where two plates are moving towards each other

Ecotourism   A type of tourism that does not do any damage to the environment and that seeks to support local communities

Emergency aid   Short-term assistance following a disaster, such as an earthquake. This might involve food, water, medicines and shelter

Epicentre   The point on the ground surface immediately above the focus of an earthquake

Epiphytes   Plants that obtain their nutrients direct from the air and therefore do not need soil. They are commonly found on tree branches in tropical rainforests

Exoskeleton   Outer skeleton of an animal

Family planning   Measures adopted to reduce the number or control the timing of children being born

Fault   A crack in a section of solid rock along which one side has moved in relation to the other

Flash flooding   Sudden flooding often resulting from a torrential storm

Flow lines   Lines on a map used to show movement between places. They can be drawn at different thicknesses to show the amount of movement taking place

Food miles   The number of miles that food items have been transported from where they have been produced to where they are being consumed or bought.

Functional areas   An area, for example part of a town, where a particular function dominates, e.g. industry or shopping

Globalisation   The trend for products, services and culture to be more worldwide, e.g. the spread of the internet and the worldwide presence of food chains such as MacDonalds

Greenhouse effect   The ability of the atmosphere to absorb heat given off from the Earth. This forms a blanket of warmth without which life on Earth would not exist

Human Development Index   A measure of development involving life expectancy, income and literacy

Hurricane warning   A warning issued to areas to expect a hurricane within the next 12 hours

Hurricane watch   A warning issued to areas at risk from a hurricane in the next 36 hours

Hydro-electric power (HEP)   Electricity generated by water flowing through turbines. Most HEP stations are in mountain areas where there are plenty of fast flowing rivers

Ice cores   A cylinder of ice taken as a core from deep within an ice sheet, e.g. in Antarctica. Ice cores are used to research climate change

Intensive farming   A type of farming that produces high yields per hectare often by using expensive inputs such as fertilisers and machinery

International time zones   Map showing relative time differences around the world

Invasive species   A species of plant or animal that becomes introduced in an area and flourishes at the expense of the native species

Kapok   A tall tree (an emergent) found in a tropical rainforest

Kyoto protocol   An international agreement to cut emissions of carbon dioxide in an attempt to reduce global warming

Labour intensive   A process, such as farming, that involves a large number of people

Lahars   A mudflow associated with a volcanic eruption

Latitude   Horizontal lines drawn around the world parallel to the Equator

Lava   Molten rock material emitted from a volcano

Living wage   The minimum amount of money considered to be enough to provide food and shelter and a reasonable quality of life

Longer-term responses   Responses to that occur in the months and years following a disaster such as an earthquake. These responses might include re-building houses and roads

Longitude   Lines drawn around the world between the north pole and the south pole. The 0 degree line of longitude passes through London

Long-term aid   Support, often provided by donor countries or charity organisations aimed to help people in poorer countries over a period of several years, e.g. education

Magma   Molten rock and gases formed deep underground

Megacities   Huge urban areas with a population in excess of 10 million people

Monsoon   A period of very heavy rain often lasting for a few weeks in places like India and Bangladesh

Mountain chains   Narrow belts of mountains extending for many hundreds of kilometres, e.g. the Andes in South America

Natural decrease   When birth rate falls below death rate there is a natural decrease in the population

Natural increase   When birth rate is above death rate there is a natural increase in the population

Nomadic pastoralism   A type of farming involving nomads who herd their animals over large areas of grassland, e.g. in parts of North Africa

Non-governmental organisations (NGOs)   Organisations, such as charities, that are not linked to the government

Ocean currents   Currents of heat flow in the world's oceans, e.g. the North Atlantic Drift

Ocean trenches   Deep gashes in the ocean floor often several thousand metres deep found at a destructive plate margin

'One-child' policy   A birth control policy introduced in China in 1979 to reduce the growth of population by limiting married couples to one child

Overfishing   Excessive unsustainable fishing that results in a reduction of fish stocks

Overgrazing   Where too many animals are grazed on an area of land resulting in long-term damage, e.g. soil erosion or desertification.

Plankton   Minute plants and animals living in the sea and forming the bottom of the food chain for a number of species

Plate margin   The edge of a tectonic plate

Plate tectonics   The theory that explains the location of major physical features such as mountain chains, volcanoes and ocean trenches

Plates   Large 'slabs' of the Earth's crust up to 100km thick

Pollution   The introduction of harmful substances into a natural environment, e.g. the pollution of oceans by oil spills or plastic waste

Polyps   The individual living organisms that collectively forms coral reefs

Population density   The number of people in an area, such as a km2

Porous   Rocks that contain pores (holes), such as chalk and sandstone

Primary producers   An organism that converts energy from the sun into energy that can be consumed by other organisms, e.g. sea grass in a coral reef ecosystem

Prime Meridian   The 0 degree line of longitude that passes through London

Projection   A method used by map makers to convert the spherical Earth into a flat map

Pyroclastic flow   An avalanche of hot rocks and gases emitted by a volcano

Quotas   An agreed limit, for example milk quotas limit the amount of milk that a farmer can produce

Refugees   People who have been forced to move away from their home country to seek safety in another country

Reservoirs   An artificial body of water held back by a dam that may be used for drinking water supply, irrigation or HEP

Resource   A product or material that is of use, for example, timber, water or people

Richter scale   The scale used to measure the magnitude (strength) of an earthquake

Sabo dams   Dams, either made of earth or concrete, used to hold back or slow down lahars (mudflows) following volcanic eruptions

Scattergraph   A graph used to plot two sets of data that are thought to be related to one another, e.g. GNP and birth rates

Seismometer   An instrument used to measure earthquakes

Short-term responses   Immediate responses often by local communities to a disaster, e.g. search and rescue and medical help

Soil erosion   The removal of fertile topsoil by wind or water

Solar ovens   Sustainable low technology devices that can be used as alternatives to firewood or paraffin cookers in poorer parts of the world

Storm surge   An increase in sea level at the coast, often in the form of high waves, caused by storms such as hurricanes

Submersibles   Equipment or forms of transportation (e.g. submarines) that can go underwater

Subsistence   A type of farming involving the production of food to feed the farmer and his/her family only

Sustainable development   Improving people's quality of life without harming the environment. Making sure that present day resources are still available for future generations

Sustainable management   Managing an environment in such a way to ensure that it is not harmed, e.g. preventing pollution and loss of habitats

Sweatshops   Factories, often making clothes, where large numbers of people are employed in poor working conditions for low wages

Thermal expansion   The physical expansion of water when it becomes heated. This is the main cause of rising sea levels associated with global warming

Time differences   Differences in time between places in different international time zones

Tropical rainforest   A type of biome found in the wet tropical regions of the world

Tsunami   One or more large waves caused by an earthquake or volcanic eruption that can result in tremendous destruction of coastal communities

Urbanisation   The increase in the proportion of people living in towns and cities

Wadis   Dry valleys found in desert regions formed by vary rare torrential rainstorms

Water cycle   The constant recycling of water involving processes such as evaporation, condensation and precipitation

Water harvesting   The collection of water from mist and fog using nets to 'harvest' water droplets from the air

Whaling   Commercial catching of whales

Wind towers   Tall towers with open window spaces to collect and circulate air. This is a traditional form of air conditioning used in hot places such as Dubai

INDEX